P9-EJT-001

Everybody's
Vegan
Cookbook

Other Books from Integral Yoga Publications:

by Sri Swami Satchidananda:

The Yoga Sutras of Patanjali
(with full commentary, Sanskrit and Index)

Integral Yoga: The Yoga Sutras of Patanjali – Pocket Edition

Integral Yoga Hatha

Beyond Words

Enlightening Tales

The Golden Present

Guru and Disciple

The Healthy Vegetarian

Kailash Journal

The Living Gita

To Know Your Self

About Swami Satchidananda:

Sri Swami Satchidananda: Apostle of Peace

Sri Swami Satchidananda: Portrait of a Modern Sage
(a pictorial biography)

The Master's Touch

Other Titles:

Imagine That! A Child's Guide to Yoga

Meditating with Children

Dictionary of Sanskrit Names

Hatha Yoga For Kids by Kids!

Lotus Prayer Book

Everybody's Vegan Cookbook

by
Ro & Joanna Piekarski

Illustrated by Gali Nahar
Cover Illustrations by Uma Schreiber

Integral Yoga® Publications
Satchidananda Ashram – Yogaville
Buckingham, Virginia

Library of Congress Cataloging-in-Publication Data

Piekarski, Ro, 1948-
Everybody's vegan cookbook / by Ro & Joanna Piekarski;
illustrated by Gali Nahar;
cover illustrations by Uma Schreiber.
    p. cm.
ISBN 0-932040-50-0 (alk. paper)
1. Vegan cookery. 2. Low-fat diet--Recipes. I. Piekarski, Joanna, 1950- II. Title.

TX837.P5292 2003
641.5' 636--dc21

                                        2003051086

WELCOME

The philosophy of thinking, eating, and living that underlies this book can be described as "dynamic harmlessness." It is an attempt to be always aware of the consequences of one's actions and to make choices that enhance well-being or, at the least, minimize detrimental impact—for oneself, other people, other creatures, all life, and planetary life support.

Everybody's Vegan Cookbook will not only lift its users to more healthful heights, but it will help guide them into a cycle of increasing vitality and more harmonious balance for ecological systems. We are confident that your culinary enjoyment will soar, your lifestyle will be invigorated, and a gentler coexistence with all life with flourish.

Using our favorite nutritious recipes, developed over the last twenty years, you can begin to attain these timeless and treasured goals. It will take no extra time, and you'll be amazed how wonderful it tastes. A whole-food, animal-free diet will subtract unwanted pounds and inches from your body, reduce the risk of life-threatening diseases associated with eating unhealthy foods, add happier years to your life, and contribute to restoring the natural environment.

In our experience, *Everybody's Vegan Cookbook* is all that is needed for eating with total health and enjoyment. Aren't our and our families' health and happiness the most important assets we ought to protect and promote? Without continued good health so much less in life can be enjoyed or accomplished. Our diet should be a long-term way of eating based on a conscious philosophy of holistic, creative thinking and living. For over twenty years the two of us have evolved our eating habits away from the typical American diet to an ethical, asthetic, plant-based, low-fat diet that we believe is unsurpassed nutritionally. The appreciation and love that permeates meal preparation is expressed in the food, absorbed with the nutrients, and radiated in compassionate living. Our vibrant good health and strength—as we enter our sixth decade—prove for us the value of this way of eating. Come join us on this essential, sound, and spirited path and share the joy and ease of delicious, deeply nourishing, environmentally friendly food.

Joanna and Ro Piekarski
Summer 2003

i

Introduction

The recipes in *Everybody's Vegan Cookbook* contain only nutritious, low-fat, whole foods derived solely from plants. They comprise a supremely healthful, wholly ethical, total-vegetarian cornucopia of scrumptious variety created entirely from whole grains, vegetables, fruits, and legumes. The *Everybody's Vegan Cookbook* approach is the key to an optimal balance of the macronutrients—complex carbohydrates, protein, and fat (approximately 75%, 15%, and 10% of calories, respectively), and of the micronutrients—amino acids, enzymes, minerals, and vitamins. This way of eating also ensures high-energy fuel and adequate fiber.

Numerous recent books and articles explain the properties of cholesterol and fats, and their deleterious effects on the body—particularly arteriosclerosis, which can lead to heart disease and stroke, and free-radical formation, which has been implicated as a precursor to cancer. Almost all the recipes in *Everybody's Vegan Cookbook* contain no added fat. Along with the absence of animals and animal products, which zeroes out intake of cholesterol (LDL), the recipes in *Everybody's Vegan Cookbook* exclude the high-fat foods margarine, shortening, and nuts. Oils and seeds, also high in fat, are minimized. Oil is needed only to coat bakeware that lacks a nonstick surface and for a few other uses. For these uses, research findings suggest virgin olive oil, sesame oil, or Canola oil. Also eliminated in *Everybody's Vegan Cookbook* are refined sweeteners, most processed foods, alcohol, and caffeine. The foods are so flavorful that salt is needless.

Everybody's Vegan Cookbook recipes use cooking methods that don't add fat and that best retain the nutrients, flavor, and appearance of fresh, raw foods. Vegetables are "sautéed" or "steam-fried" in a small amount of water or steamed over water in a covered pan just until crisp-tender.

With no grease to clean up, a fat-free kitchen requires less hot water. Milder herbal dishwashing liquid, free of toxins, will do the job. And with a plant-based diet, food contamination concerns, which primarily involve meat and animal products, are drastically reduced.

Please don't think you have to follow exactly the ingredients, amounts, and procedures suggested in *Everybody's Vegan Cookbook* recipes. Adapt them to your preferences and circumstances, what's in season from different geographic regions, what you have on hand, and what your intuition and prior experience suggest. Just as an infinite number of unique sentences can be created from a large but finite number of words in any language, an infinite number of delicious dishes can be created from a large but finite number of healthful ingredients. Evolve the recipes into your own style, change them each time to suit season, location, and mood, but don't devolve them by reverting to unhealthy components from which many of the ideas were originally converted!

Prep times are variable, depending on your pace, time and tools available, and whether a recipe is prepared all at once or in stages. You can approximate a schedule for yourself when you read through a recipe.

Number of servings can't be accurately specified, either. Is the recipe going to be used as a first course, side dish, or main event? Who are the eaters and how hungry are they?

Nutritional analyses are also superfluous with Everybody's Vegan Cookbook recipes. If you adhere to *Everybody's Vegan Cookbook* guidelines, your body will luxuriate in the ultimate in healthful, balanced nutrition.

Some ingredients may be unfamiliar, but all are worth getting to know. Browse around a natural foods coop or store and select something new to try. Soon previously unknown foods will be welcome additions to your cooking repertoire.

The Basics chapter is intended as a reference as you prepare meals that taste great and that you can feel good about in every way.

CONTENTS

THE BASICS

GRAINS

Amaranth is the tiny, high-protein seed of an ancient, fast-growing, tall, cereal-like plant cultivated for centuries in tropical and temperate climates worldwide. The cooked seeds have a glutinous texture and a delicate, nutty flavor.

Use 3 cups water for every 1 cup amaranth (amaranth will triple).

Place amaranth and water in a pot and bring to a boil. Stir, reduce to a simmer, cover, and cook about 30 minutes, until all the water is absorbed.

Barley is a delicious, chewy grain often associated with warming, filling wintertime soups. Buy hulled barley, the whole grain with only the inedible outer layers removed, at a natural foods coop or store. (Supermarkets have the less-nutritious pearled barley.) Like all whole grains, barley is a good source of fiber and protein. It's also high in the B-vitamins niacin and thiamine, and in minerals, especially calcium, phosphorous, and potassium.

Use 3 cups water for every 1 cup barley (barley will more than triple).

Place barley and water in a pot and bring to a boil. Reduce to a simmer, cover, and cook about 1½ hours, until barley is soft and all the water is absorbed.

Brown Rice is a staple food for more than half the earth's population. Brown rice is the whole rice kernel with hull removed and bran intact, so it's naturally more nutritious than milled (white) rice, containing abundant B-vitamins, vitamin E, minerals, and fiber. Cooked long-grain rice kernels are separate and fluffy; medium-grain are more soft and tender; short-grain brown rice and waxy short-grain sweet brown rice contain more starchy gluten, so they're stickier when cooked.

Use 2 cups water for every 1 cup rice (rice will double).

Mix rice and water in a pot, bring to a boil, reduce heat, cover and simmer 45 minutes, until all water is absorbed. Turn off heat and let sit another 15 minutes. Don't stir.

Buckwheat Groats (Kasha) are the reddish-brown three-cornered seeds of the bush-like buckwheat plant, which is technically not a grain, though it looks and cooks like one. Cooked as kasha, buckwheat has a unique, hearty flavor and is rich in the B-vitamins thiamine and riboflavin and the minerals calcium, phosphorus, and potassium.

Use 2 cups water for every 1 cup buckwheat (kasha will more than double).

Boil water, stir in kasha, reduce heat to very low, cover, and simmer 15 minutes, until all water is absorbed.

Bulgur Wheat is a quick-to-prepare form of whole wheat, made by steaming then drying wheat berries, removing some of the bran layers, and cracking them into several pieces. Bulgur has the same nutrients as whole wheat but in smaller quantities: protein, B-vitamins, iron, and phosphorous.

Use 2 cups water for every 1 cup bulgur (bulgur will more than double).

Boil water in a teapot. Place bulgur in a pot. Pour boiling water over bulgur, stir once, cover, and let sit about 20 minutes, until all water is absorbed. Bulgur should be light and fluffy.

Couscous is finely cracked, steamed, and dried wheat. Cooked, it's golden-brown, light and fluffy, with a sweet, mild taste. It's the fastest of all grains to prepare and one of the most versatile.

Use 3 cups water for every 1 cup couscous (couscous will triple).

Boil water in a teapot. Place couscous in a pot. Pour boiling water over couscous, stir once, cover, and let sit about 15 minutes, until couscous is soft and fluffy and all water is absorbed.

Or, pour any temperature water over couscous, cover, and let sit about 1 hour, until all water is absorbed.

Millet, the pale, round grain, has a distinct, gentle flavor. Millet is high in B-vitamins, protein, and minerals, including potassium, and low in sodium.

Use 2 cups water for every 1 cup millet (millet will more than triple).

Place millet and water in a pot and bring to a boil. Reduce to a simmer, cover, and cook about 30 minutes, until millet is soft and all water is absorbed.

Oats have been eaten in North America since the colonists first planted it in the 1600s. Rolled oats, those sweet, light flakes, are hulled, heated, and pressed whole kernels (groats) of the oat grain. They're less nutritious than hulled groats, but since the bran and germ remain intact in processing, both rolled oats and oat groats are rich in B vitamins, vitamin E, phosphorous, iron, and copper.

Rolled oats (raw or cooked) and oat bran are breakfast staples, and along with oat flour, are components of some breads and desserts. Rolled oats vary widely in size and texture; some are very soft, others firm. For breakfast, let preference guide you, but softer oats are better for baking and make creamier oatmeal.

To cook oat groats, stir 1 cup groats into every 2 cups boiling water. Cover, reduce heat to low, and simmer 45 minutes. (Oats will double.)

To cook rolled oats, stir 1 cup rolled oats into every 2 cups boiling water. Return to a boil, reduce heat, cover, and simmer a few minutes, stirring occasionally.

Quinoa ("keen-wa"), along with corn and potatoes, was a staple food of the Inca civilization. It's the highest of all grains in protein, and its protein is complete and amino-acid balanced. It also contains other vital nutrients: fiber, minerals, and vitamins. It has a pleasing taste, and it's light, versatile, and quick to prepare. Though expensive, it expands more than other grains during cooking.

Use 2 cups water for every 1 cup quinoa (quinoa will quadruple).

Rinse the quinoa by using a strainer, or placing in a pot, covering with water, and draining.

Place rinsed quinoa and water in a pot and bring to a boil. Reduce to a simmer, cover, and cook 10-15 minutes, until the grains are translucent and all the water is absorbed.

Spelt is a 9000-year-old grain that first grew wild in mountain valleys of the Middle East and Europe. The whole grain is similar to wheat berries, but its gluten is more fragile and easily broken down, so it cooks more quickly and baked goods made with spelt flour are lighter and more delicate in taste and texture.

Use 2 cups water for every 1 cup spelt grain (spelt will double in volume).

Place spelt and water in a pot and bring to a boil. Reduce to a simmer, cover, and cook about an hour, until fully soft and all the water is absorbed.

Teff, an ancient, versatile grain from Ethiopia, is rich in vitamin B-1, iron, and calcium. With its mild, slightly molasses-like sweetness, uncooked teff can be added to baked desserts and puddings or substituted for nuts or other seeds. Cooked teff, which is gelatinous and full-bodied, is a good thickener for soups, stews, and casseroles. Teff can be cooked in combination with other grains, such as brown rice, buckwheat groats, corn meal, couscous, and millet.

Use 3 cups water for every 1 cup teff seed (teff will triple in volume).

Boil the water, add teff, return to a boil, then cover and simmer about 15 minutes, or until all water is absorbed.

Wheat Berries (whole wheat kernels) are the most nutritious form of wheat. In their entirety of bran, germ, and complex carbohydrates, they contain protein, B-vitamins, vitamin E, iron, and fiber.

Use 3 cups water for every 1 cup wheat berries (wheat berries will almost triple in volume).

Place wheat berries and water in a pot and bring to a boil. Reduce to a simmer, cover, and cook 2 hours, until wheat berries are soft and all the water is absorbed.

FLOUR

Stone-ground whole-wheat flour, with the wheat germ, bran, and fiber of the whole wheat grain crushed but preserved, is basic to healthful baking. Stone-ground whole-wheat bread flour and pastry flour are available in bulk in natural foods coops and stores. Pastry flour is made from softer wheat than bread flour and is more finely milled.

Flours ground from other grains—amaranth, barley, buckwheat, corn, millet, oats, rice, rye, soy, spelt, teff, triticale (a cross between wheat and rye)—add variety to your breads, muffins, biscuits, desserts, and pancakes. A hand or electric grain mill means none-fresher flour with the heartiest flavor from any grain.

BEANS

To cook any type of beans, place in a pot with plenty of water, cover, bring to boil, turn down the heat, and simmer until soft but still shapely, tender but not mushy. Two ways to reduce cooking times are to soak the beans all day or overnight, or to boil a minute or two, then soak an hour. Drain and rinse after soaking.

Here are the amounts of water to use for each cup of unsoaked dry beans and their approximate cooking times and yields:

	water	*time*	*yield*
aduki beans	3 cups	2 hours	2 cups
black beans	4 cups	1½ hours	2 cups
chickpeas (garbanzo beans)	4 cups	3 hours	4 cups
kidney beans	3 cups	1½ hours	2½ cups
lentils	3 cups	1 hour	3 cups
lima beans	2 cups	1½ hours	1½ cups
navy beans	2 cups	1½ hours	2½ cups
pinto beans	3 cups	2½ hours	2 cups
soybeans	3 cups	3 hours	2 cups
soy grits	4 cups	15 minutes	2 cups
split peas	3 cups	1 hour	2½ cups

Canned beans can be used in place of those you cook yourself, but it's not easy to find them additive-free, except at natural foods coops and stores. One can contains about 1½ cups of drained beans.

"Beano" is a food enzyme preparation that "almost always prevents gas from forming." Sprinkle about five drops on the first bite of foods that cause "gasiness and embarrassment." Find Beano at natural foods coops and stores, supermarkets, and drug stores.

SOY FOODS

Soybeans are an excellent source of protein, with a good balance of essential amino acids, and they can be transformed into an array of nutritious foods with vastly different tastes, textures, and uses. Soy milk, soy yogurt, and soy "cream cheese" can be made relatively easily at home, and many soy foods are staples at natural foods stores and coops, and, of course, Oriental markets. Some can be found in large supermarkets.

Tofu

Tofu, also known as soybean curd or soy cheese, is a traditional natural soy food of the East that's perfect for nutrition-, taste-, environment- and cost-conscious people of the West. First, soymilk is made by heating and puréeing soaked soybeans, then separating the liquid from the solids. The soymilk is then curdled with the addition of nigari—the minerals from desalinated sea water, calcium sulfate (from gypsum), magnesium sulfate (Epsom salts), vinegar, or lemon juice—and solidified by pressing.

Once you become familiar with tofu's remarkable versatility, simplicity of use, healthfulness, and its mild flavor—which encourages an infinite variety of combinations with other foods, you'll find it's indispensable to your cooking repertoire. Tofu is widely available, in natural foods coops and stores and Oriental markets, and in produce markets and supermarkets, in several forms: soft, firm, or extra-firm, even "lite". It comes fresh in bulk, in long-keeping sealed plastic tubs and wrappers, and in even longer-keeping small airtight aseptic packages of "silken" (firm yet creamy) tofu. Or, in less than an hour, you can make your own at home.

Storing Tofu

Store tofu covered with water in a covered container in the refrigerator. Every few days, drain and rinse the tofu, and re-cover it with cold water. If you buy tofu in the 1-lb plastic tubs, keep sealed until you're ready to use it. Transfer the unused portion to another container for storage. (The tofu tubs have a recycling code of "2," which means they're accepted anywhere plastic can be brought for recycling.)

Pressing tofu

Pressing removes water equal to about 30% of the tofu's weight, resulting in much firmer tofu that keeps its form during preparation and more fully absorbs flavors from other foods.

Cut a block of tofu into slices of equal thickness. Place the pieces at one end of a kitchen towel. Fold the towel over the tofu and cover with a cutting board or baking sheet. Place a heavy object, such as a rock, a pot filled with water, bean- or grain-filled jars, or a 5-pound bag of onions, on top. Press at least ½ hour. If you plan to press it for a long time, set the towel on a board or plate and refrigerate.

Crumbling tofu

Crumbling removes twice as much water as pressing, resulting in a firm, light, fluffy texture.

Combine 12 oz tofu and 1 cup water in a pan. Break the tofu into small pieces with a fork or wooden spoon while bringing the water to a boil. Reduce heat and simmer 1-2 minutes. Place a cloth- or towel-lined colander in the sink. Pour in the tofu mixture, twist the cloth or towel closed, and use a masher or jar to press out as much water as possible.

Empty the tofu into a bowl, let cool, and break into very small pieces with spoon or fingertips.

Squeezing tofu

This process results in a mashed tofu that is slightly cohesive, with a cottage-cheese texture.

Place tofu at the center of a dry dishtowel. Twist the towel closed and squeeze firmly, but lightly enough that no tofu penetrates the cloth. Knead for 2-3 minutes to expel as much water as possible.

Freezing tofu

When tofu is frozen, its water content (about 86%) turns to ice and the remaining essence of tofu forms a sponge-like, crystalline network of high-quality protein. Frozen tofu is resilient, cohesive, and absorbent. Its unique flavor is enhanced by the other flavors it readily absorbs when simmered. It's a good way to make use of tofu that you won't be able to use before it's no longer fresh.

Cut a pound block of tofu into ⅜-inch-thick slices and arrange in one layer on a plate or baking sheet, or in several layers between sheets of waxed paper (perhaps reused waxed bags from breakfast cereal boxes), taking care that the tofu pieces don't touch. Place in the freezer for at least 48 hours, up to several months. The longer the better; texture improves with storage time. Remove from plate or sheet and store frozen in a sealed bag. For faster freezing, place tofu slices in a protected location outside at -20°F, then place in the indoor freezer.

To reconstitute, place frozen tofu in a large bowl or pot. Cover with boiling water and let stand until soft. Pour off hot water and re-cover with cold water. Lift out each piece and gently but firmly press between both hands to expel most of the water.

Refreshing tofu

In the unlikely event that your stored tofu shows signs of spoiling, you can quickly refresh it by parboiling.

Boil a quart of water, reduce heat to low, and drop in the tofu whole or cut into sections. Cover and heat for 2-3 m minutes, until the tofu is well warmed. Lift out the finished pieces with a slotted spoon.

OTHER PREPARED SOY FOODS

Miso is an enzyme-fermented soybean paste condiment made from cooked, aged soybeans. Other ingredients, such as rice, barley, or chickpeas, and aging times ranging from a few months to a few years, result in a variety of flavors—mild, subtle, mellow, or strong; light, rich, or deep; and sweet or salty; and the colors are a palette of earth tones.

Soy grits or granules, made from toasted coarsely ground soybeans, have a delicious nutty flavor and a cooking time one-twelfth that of whole soybeans. They're a hearty and nutritious addition to soups and grain and vegetable dishes.

Soy flour is made by grinding whole dry or roasted soybeans, just as whole wheat kernels are ground into flour. To boost the protein content of bread or pancakes, you can use part soy flour, but you may prefer...

Soy powder, which is made by drying and grinding cooked, hulled soybeans. Soy powder has a finer texture and a more pleasant flavor than soy flour. Soy powder can be used in casseroles and baking, and stirred into soup and hot carob and grain beverages to make them "creamy." For plain soy milk, add 1 part soy powder to 4 parts water and stir well. But the taste can't compare to that of real homemade soymilk (p. 9) or the many brands and types of delicious prepared soy beverages.

Soymilk is the common name for the variety of soy beverages that have been proliferating in natural foods coops and stores. Soymilk is made by soaking soybeans, grinding and heating them, then pressing out the liquid. Plain, vanilla, and carob soymilk are all lightly sweetened with rice syrup or barley malt. Check the ingredients; some contain oil. Also check the nutrition information panel.; fat content varies among brands and flavors. ("Light" styles are lowest in fat.) Soy beverage concentrates reduce cost and packaging. Soymilk containers are recyclable.

Soy yogurt has the beneficial bacillus cultures of regular yogurt, without the dairy.

Tamari (shoyu) is the natural form of synthetic, additive-ridden "soy sauce." Tamari is fermented from soybeans, water, salt, wheat, and a yeast culture for several months or longer. It's also available "lite," with lower sodium content.

Tempeh is a "cultured" soyfood made by a natural fermentation process like that used for bread, yogurt, miso, and tamari. Whole, cooked soybeans are bound together by a cottony spore into a dense, chewy cake that's ready to eat on a spur-of-the-moment TLT (tempeh, lettuce, and tomato) sandwich, or cooked in a more elaborate recipe as the main course of a delicious, satisfying, *Think Eat Live* dinner.

Texturized Vegetable Protein (TVP) is a dried granular food prepared from defatted soy flakes, and sometimes seasoned with tamari. It's quick cooking, and its tastelessness is an asset: It goes well with any vegetables and herbs, and absorbs flavors well. It can be used, for example, in "sloppy Joes," chili, and tomato sauce. For 2 cups of reconstituted ready-to-eat chewy TVP, combine 1 cup of dry TVP with ⅞ cup tap water or boiling water, stir, and soak for 10 minutes.

SOY FOODS YOU CAN MAKE AT HOME

Soymilk

Wash and drain 1 cup soybeans three times. Soak in 2 quarts water for 10 hours, then rinse and drain twice. Line a colander with a large moistened 2-foot-square towel, or even better, a 15- by 15-inch sack made by folding in half a coarsely woven cotton dishtowel or piece of linen and sewing three edges together. Set the colander in a pot or large bowl.

Heat 1 cup of water over low heat in a covered pot. While water is heating, combine soaked beans and 2⅔ cup water in a blender or processor and purée until very smooth, about 30 seconds.

Add purée to the heating (or boiling) water. Rinse the blender or processor with ¼ cup water and pour the remaining purée into the pot. Increase heat to medium-high and stir constantly for a few minutes, until foam suddenly rises in the pot.

Turn off the heat and pour the contents into the prepared colander, using a spatula to scrape out every bit. Twist the towel or sack closed and press firmly with a masher or jar to expel the soymilk, finally squeezing by hand to extract as much soymilk as possible.

Pour the soymilk into a pot and bring to a boil over medium-high heat, stirring constantly. Reduce heat and cook about 6 minutes.

The soybean pulp that remains in the towel or sack is called okara.*

Use soy milk to make soy yogurt (p. 10) or in other recipes, or drink hot or cold, perhaps sweetened with rice syrup, (about 2 tsp per cup) seasoned with ginger and nutmeg (⅛ tsp each per cup), and flavored with carob powder (1 level tblsp per cup). For a soymilkshake, purée in a blender or processor with fresh fruit, rice syrup, and perhaps a dash of nutmeg.

Soymilk can be transformed into tofu by a beautiful process detailed in *The Book of Tofu* by William Shurtleff and Akiko Aoyagi.

*Okara

This by-product of making soymilk (and tofu) is a nutritious, high-fiber food in its own right. See pages 22, 83, 136, and 215 for some suggestions for its use.

Soy Yogurt

Use low-fat, low-calorie soy yogurt in place of mayonnaise, sour cream, whipped cream, and other high-fat and cholesterol foods that people and the planet are much better off without, and as a delicious, creamy addition to many recipes and food combinations. Use it to make an excellent substitute for cream cheese (see p. 11).

Have all utensils very clean: wash with hot soapy water, and rinse with boiling water.

Pour a batch of homemade soymilk or a one-liter container of plain soymilk—sweetened or unsweetened—into a pan, or place 1 cup soy powder in the pan and slowly stir in 1 quart water.

Heat carefully to lukewarm ("baby bottle" temperature—test with your wrist). If you have a thermometer, the ideal temperature is 110°-118°F (43°-48°C). If the soymilk is too hot, the live yogurt cultures will be killed; if it's too cool, they'll remain inactive.

Pour about ½ cup of the warm soymilk into a small bowl. Add one of these yogurt starters: 1 tsp dairy-free powdered lactobacillus acidophilus or bifidus culture—for very tangy yogurt, use 1 tsp of each (available at natural foods coops and stores as a food supplement to restore or maintain healthy intestinal flora); the contents of a packet of yogurt starter; 2 tblsp of yogurt from your last batch; or ¼ cup of White Wave Dairyless (the only commercially available plain soy yogurt).

Stir well , then pour back into the pan and stir thoroughly. (A few teaspoons of agar or kanten stirred in now will help ensure successful solidification.) Put in a covered container, keep it at room temperature (optimally about 70° or slightly higher), and don't disturb it for 6-16 hours, depending on temperature.

For confident incubation, "Yogotherm" is a low-tech, zero-energy yogurt maker, consisting of an inner removable plastic container and an insulted outer container. It's like a thermos, which can also be used if your house isn't warm enough. There are many inventive ways, similar to those used for rising bread, to keep incubating yogurt warm: a protected, south-facing location outdoors on a sunny summer day; a sunny spot behind a south-facing window; near a radiator or behind a wood stove (turn very gently a few times); atop an oil burner, radiant-heat floor, register, or heating pad set to medium; in a pre-warmed oven, carefully rewarmed as needed. If you're not using a yogurt maker, it's a good idea to protect the yogurt in a temperature-modulating warm-water jacket. For example, a tightly capped quart canning jar filled with inoculated soymilk can be immersed in warm water in a watertight covered canister.

When the yogurt is ready, put it in the refrigerator; it will firm up a bit more. Remember to set 2 tblsp aside for your next batch.

If you started with unsweetened soymilk, you can sweeten the yogurt by blending in fruit or all-fruit preserves, or vanilla and rice syrup, when the yogurt is fully cultured and cold. Soy yogurt can be mixed with juice and fruit to make frozen "soygurt" - see p. 209.

Soy Cream Cheese

Place fresh soy yogurt in several layers of cheesecloth, tie it securely (a bag twister works well), and place it in a strainer or colander. Place a bowl under it to collect the whey, and set a weight, such as a rock or jar of beans, on top. Or, place fresh soy yogurt in a small boiled cotton bag, and improvise a way to hang it over a bowl. Either way, keep in the refrigerator for 6 to 24 hours. The longer you leave it, the thicker the "cheese" and the sharper the taste.

Use it plain, or stir in some seasonings, such as basil, cayenne, curry, dill, garlic, hot sauce, lemon juice, marjoram, mustard, finely chopped chives or onions, parsley, or black or white pepper.

The volume will be reduced by half, but you'll also have the whey, which you can use in baking, hot or cold cereal, or soup.

SPROUTS

Sprouted seeds are easy-to-grow, versatile, delicious, inexpensive, and nutritious greens, especially welcome in the winter months, when they can fill in for garden lettuce. Fluffy sprouts, such as red clover and alfalfa, swell winter salads and sandwiches. Firmer sprouts, such as radish, wheat berry, mung, and lentil, can also be tossed in salads, and added to stir-fries during the last couple of minutes.

When you provide a few tablespoons of seeds in a sprouter with their basic needs—moisture, warmth, and darkness, their volume will increase prodigiously. Moisture comes from initial soaking and twice-daily rinsing. If you filter your water for drinking or buy drinking water, use that for your sprouts, too. Room temperature suffices for warmth. Keep them in the dark by covering with a dishtowel. You can buy a sprouter or improvise one using either a glass jar or an opaque casserole dish.

For the jar sprouter, a one-quart mason jar works well. Soak 2 tablespoons of seeds in the jar in a cup of warm water all day or overnight. Plastic sprouting caps that fit wide-mouth mason jars are available at natural foods coops and stores. Using those or a square of cheesecloth, nylon mesh, or screening held over the top with a rubber band or canning ring, you can empty the water right from the jar. Or, you can drain the seeds with a strainer and then return them to the jar. Lay the jar on its side on your counter, covered with a dishtowel. Then, twice daily—morning and evening—rinse by covering the sprouting seeds with warm water and draining thoroughly.

For the casserole sprouter, first soak the seeds in a smaller container and drain. Spread them on the bottom of a casserole dish and place a damp towel over the top. Rinse twice daily by covering with warm water and draining through a strainer. Keep the towel moist.

Sprouts are usually ready in about 3-5 days, depending on temperature. Some sprouts become bitter if they get too long. Fluffy sprouts will fill the jar (about

1-2 inches in length); bean sprouts are best at ½ to 1 inch (mung can get even longer); grains and sesame and sunflower seeds are ready at ½ inch or less. In general, other sprouts are good at about one inch. Store sprouts in the refrigerator.

Green plants are the only organisms on Earth that can make food; chlorophyll in plants in the presence of sunlight initiates photosynthesis. When your sprouts are ready, place them briefly in a sunny spot. If they're in a jar, turn occasionally until all sides are green. Their nutritional and aesthetic value increase as they green up. Soy and sunflower sprouts, however, become bitter in sunlight.

Sprouting enables use of hard seeds as nutritious food without cooking. Sprouted seeds contain all the nutrients the plant needs to grow: vitamins (especially A, Bs, and C), minerals (especially iron and calcium), enzymes, protein, and fiber.

The list of other seeds that can be sprouted is naturally very long. It includes cress, kale, lettuce, mustard, beet, cabbage, corn, onion, pea, caraway, celery, dill, parsley, barley, buckwheat, millet, oat, rye, flax, pumpkin, sesame, sunflower, garbanzo, lima, pinto, soy, and other beans. Seed mixes are also available, or you can make your own combinations.

Many garden seeds are chemically treated. Use only untreated seeds and those sold at natural foods coops and stores, which are intended for sprouting. Don't use potato, tomato, or apple seeds; they're toxic.

SWEETENERS

Most of the recipes in *Everybody's Vegan Cookbook* use brown rice syrup as sweetener. Rice syrup contains rice, water, and natural cereal enzymes. Rice syrup and barley malt (which is thicker and harder to work with) contain complex sugars, which are metabolized in the body more slowly than the simple sugars of other sweeteners, without triggering a quick rise in blood sugar levels, a mineral- and vitamin-deficit reaction, and an energy-draining shock.

Dry sweeteners—brown rice syrup powder, apple fiber powder, and date sugar—are a bit more convenient, but they're hard to find and expensive. You can make your own date sugar: Bake unfloured dry date pieces in a low oven until completely desiccated and brittle. Allow to cool, then pulverize in a food processor.

Sometimes the only sweetener a recipe needs is fruit or fruit juice. This is a good use for the liquid from soaked dried fruit or cooked fresh fruit.

Each recipe suggests a minimum amount of sweetener. This way, everyone is happy: Those who prefer their food less sweet will like it as is, and those who like it sweeter can add more.

OTHER FOODS THAT MAY BE UNFAMILIAR

Agar (kanten) is a natural plant gelatin derived from sea vegetables, available in bars, strands, flakes, and powder.

Arrowroot and **kuzu** are ground vegetable-root powders used like cornstarch as thickeners. Use ⅓ more kuzu than cornstarch, ⅔ as much arrowroot as cornstarch, or half as much arrowroot as kuzu.

Carob (St. John's bread) is a caffeine-free chocolate substitute in powdered form, made from the seed of a tree-borne pod.

Mirin is a naturally sweet, mellow, golden-colored clear liquid seasoning made from steamed sweet rice and water. Use it in place of sherry or sake or to thin and flavor sauces and marinades.

Sea vegetables, containing abundant amounts of minerals, vitamins, and protein, have been a healthful staple food of Pacific Islanders and the Far East for millennia. Dried sea vegetables—arame, dulse, hijiki, kombu (kelp), nori, wakame—are available in natural foods coops and stores. They can all be broken into pieces for use in soup and stew; they expand when soaked. Store in an air-tight container after opening the package.

Shiitake and other dried mushrooms are a convenient and delicious substitute for fresh mushrooms. Their shelf life in a sealed or resealed bag is virtually indefinite. To reconstitute, soak until soft in warm water or stock for several hours, depending on size and thickness. Some varieties may take as long as 5 hours, and some have woody stems that should be cut off after soaking. They expand very little during soaking.

Tahini is a creamy purée of hulled sesame seeds that adds flavor, body, and protein to sauces, dressings, and spreads. If the oil has separated and risen to the top of the jar, you can stir it back in or pour it off into a small container and use it to coat nonstick pans, etc.

PRODUCE

There's a bit of art and science to choosing recipes and ingredients according to season and location. The harvest continuum from your own garden or a local farmer's market or farm stand is a primary guide to meal planning. At the supermarket, appearance and price are clues to the freshness of produce. For most produce, the more recently and closer to home it was picked, the better it tastes and the more nutrients it retains.

The other planning variable is what's on hand—making felicitous use of produce remnants and rotating through produce you canned or froze, matching them with other staples on the shelf and appealing recipes in the book.

Produce is precious. Beet stems, the upper parts of broccoli and cauliflower stems, even the softer parts of cabbage cores, celery leaves, and scallion tops are examples of vegetable parts that are often wasted. For Earth's sake, compost inedible parts. Save vegetable-steaming liquid to improve another recipe's flavor and nutrition by using stock instead of water, or for the next time you water-sauté.

The chemicals named on some produce cartons make shocking reading; that's a big reason why...

Organic is best

The most immediate reason for buying organic produce is for you and your family to enjoy health-promoting, delicious food that is safe from harmful insecticides, herbicides, and fungicides. In a broader view, organic farming preserves drinking-water quality, protects farmworkers from poisons, improves soil health and helps prevent soil erosion, saves energy, helps small farmers, and promotes biodiversity.

SOME OTHER NOTES ON PRODUCE

bay leaves

Don't eat them.

bell peppers

This term is used to mean sweet (not hot) peppers of any color— green, yellow, or red, or even gold, orange, brown, purple, or lavender.

ginger

Fresh ginger root stores wonderfully in the freezer. Buy a piece of fresh root, cut it into smaller sections, place them in a small plastic bag in the freezer, and call on them as needed. They are very easy to grate in their frozen state.

herbs

To dry fresh aromatic herbs such as basil, oregano, parsley, sage, and savory:

Pull out the plant and cut off the roots. Rinse clean, shake off water, and place on a towel to let surface moisture evaporate. Then gather in bunches and place each bunch in a large paper bag. Tie the mouth of the bag around the stems and place in a warm, dry, airy room, until the leaves are brittle and crumble readily.

lemon and limes

You'll get more out of lemons and limes if you squeeze out all the juice with a hand or electric juicer and funnel it into a narrow bottle that has an inner cap with a pouring slit. It'll be conveniently on hand whenever you need it, for your carbonated water at dinner or whenever called for in a recipe.

onions

Vidalia onions are more pleasant to work with; they don't cause eye irritation. Their mild flavor is appreciated by some, not onion-sharp enough for others.

Scallions, the name used throughout the book, and green onions are two names for the same member of the onion family.

potatoes

Store potatoes in darkness, since light causes potatoes to turn green. Cut off any green areas and sprouted eyes before using.

While potato skins are nutritious, they contain tannin, an astringent which you may not want to subject your digestive system to.

squash, summer and winter

Dark green zucchini, yellow crook- and straightneck, and pale green pattypan reach a peak of plenty in late July and August, and then recede. Though these can grow to mega-size, small to medium are the most tasty and tender.

The equally prolific winter squash—acorn, buttercup, butternut, delicata, Hokkaido, Hubbard, spaghetti, turban, turbanless, and others, including pumpkins—if properly stored in a dry area with good air circulation at about 50°F, can be a produce staple right through the winter.

AMELIORATIONS

You don't have to abandon your other cookbooks or accumulated recipe files to become a total-health cook. When you've become accustomed to using healthful ingredients and techniques, you can revise former favorite recipes by omitting or replacing their unwholesome components. Here are some unhealthy-to-healthy conversions:

INSTEAD OF	USE
dairy	
milk or milk powder	soymilk or soy powder (p. 5, 8, 9)
sour cream, dairy yogurt	soy yogurt (p. 8, 9, 10)
cream cheese	soy cream cheese (p. 11)
whipped cream	tofu whipped cream (p. 202)
mayonnaise	tofu mayonnaise (p. 147)
eggs	2 oz tofu or ¼ cup cooked tapioca (p. 200)
(usually, just omit)	
in baking	
white flour	stone-ground whole-wheat bread or pastry flour
chocolate	carob
oil, margarine, shortening	omit (except for small amounts of sesame or Canola oil in piecrusts)
baking powder, baking soda	reduce
refined sweeteners	rice syrup, barley malt, date sugar, apple fiber powder, fruit (see p. 12)
salt	omit, except a small amount in yeast bread
general	
white rice or pasta	whole-grain brown rice or pasta
salt	tamari, miso, herbs
oil, margarine, shortening	omit (use water to stir-fry)

EQUIPMENT

These are the kitchen essentials that you'll use constantly.

FOR FOOD PREP

bowls

one or more sets of mixing bowls, for a range of sizes from tiny to huge

cutting boards

a medium-to-large board for vegetables and
   a medium one for fruit
   (to keep garlic away from
   peaches), each with a
   non-porous surface and
   a slightly raised edge
a smaller wooden board for
   slicing bread

knives

for most chopping, cutting, and slicing:
   a medium-weight rectangular-blade cleaver-
   type knife, or a heavy 6- to 10-inch chef's
   or utility knife
a larger rectangular-blade cleaver for working
   with winter squash
and other heavy-duty jobs
a long, serrated bread knife
a paring knife for small tasks

others

apple corer, heavy cooking fork, garlic press
grater (4-sided, stainless steel), hand citrus juicer
mushroom brush (use it dry and dry it between washings)
potato masher, scissors
rubber spatula (for getting out every bit)
vegetable brush, vegetable peeler
thermometer (for making soy yogurt)

FOR MEASURING

heat-proof glass liquid measuring cups: cup, pint, and quart
set of dry measuring cups: ⅛, ¼, ⅓, ½, and 1 cup
set of measuring spoons: ⅛, ¼, ½, and 1 tsp; ½ tblsp (equal to 1½ tsp);
and 1 tblsp (3 tsp)

FOR COOKING

tea kettle for fast boiling and safe pouring of water
heavy-duty nonstick or glass saucepans *(not aluminum)* of different sizes, with covers
steamers that fit your pots and pans
a nonstick Dutch oven
wooden spoons; plastic- or nylon-coated slotted
    spoon and flipper (to protect your non-
    stick cookware)
nylon scouring pads (to clean your non-
    stick cookware)
a large (at least 6-quart) stainless steel
    pot for pasta and soup
colander and strainer
soup ladle
tongs
timer
can opener
    (Since it's used so rarely, you can get by
    with an 89¢ P-45 from an Army surplus
    store.)

FOR BAKING

several covered casseroles
nonstick 9- by 2-inch and 8- by 2-inch round and square baking pans
9-inch pie pans
9- by-5- by 3-inch loaf pans,
and some miniature ones for giving fresh loaves of bread as gifts
1 or 2 12-cup muffin tins
rolling pin, or use a cylindrical quart canning jar
12- by 15-inch nonstick baking pan
pot holders

FOR HERBS AND SPICES

little labeled storage jars

Herbs and spices bought in bulk at a natural foods coop or store cost a tiny fraction of the ones in jars and small tins at the supermarket. And, you can easily dry your own garden herbs (see p. 21). Make sure your jars have opening large enough for at least a half-teaspoon measuring spoon. Collect some with removable inner caps with shaker holes—for cinnamon, celery seed, oregano, and paprika, for example.

mortar and pestle or spice mill

Crushing and grinding spices, herbs, and seeds releases their aromas and flavors.

pepper mill

Fill with peppercorns for freshly ground black pepper.

FOR FOOD STORAGE

canisters

...or other well-sealed containers for flours and cornmeal

canning jars

half-pint, pint, quart, and larger jars for other dry goods, such as beans, grains, pasta, carob powder, soy powder, tapioca, sprouting seeds, vegetable broth powder, baking soda

narrow-necked jars

... for vinegars and tamari. Keep a large one for each, to refill at the coop, and a small one to refill (with a funnel) from the large one for at-table use.

plastic containers with lids

...saved from miso or other foods that aren't available in bulk, to reuse for refrigerating and freezing, with masking tape and a pen for labeling.

APPLIANCES

food processor
The discs slice or shred produce instantly, and the metal blade is ideal for chopping and pulverizing, and blending to total smoothality.

toaster oven
It's more versatile than a toaster for toasting different types and thicknesses of bread, and for making cinnamon toast, and it saves energy when you have something small to bake, broil, or reheat.

juicer
A masticating juicer extracts more nutrition and flavor from fruits and vegetables than a centrifugal type.

Save the by-products: vegetable pulp for use in salads, burgers, casseroles, etc.; fruit pulp for dessert recipes.

Grain mill attachments are available with some juicers.

appliances you're sure to use often, if you have them
soda syphon, frozen-dessert maker, and hot-air popcorn popper

BREAKFAST

COLD CEREAL

HOT CEREAL

BREADFAST

PANCAKES

COLD CEREAL

OATS

1. Put raw rolled oats in a bowl. Top with currants or raisins. Add orange juice, any other fruit juice, and/or soymilk or soy yogurt (p.10), or just pure cold water. Softer rolled oats will create "oat milk" that blends creamily with the juice, soymilk, or water.
2. You can also add crunchy wheat and barley cereal, shredded wheat, plain puffed cereals*, or other unsweetened cereals from the coop or natural foods store, and any kind of fruit.
3. For extra nutrition, sprinkle on ¼ teaspoon each crystalline vitamin C and spirulina, a nutrient-rich blue-green algae.

Caution: This can be habit forming.

*Beware! Every other box or bag in the supermarket cereal aisle actually contains breakfast candy.

OKARA GRANOLA

Combine 2 cups okara (p. 9) with 2 tblsp rice syrup and 1 tsp vanilla. Spread the mixture on a nonstick baking sheet and bake at 325° for 30-40 minutes, stirring occasionally, until nicely browned, crumbly, and heavenly aromatic.

HOT CEREAL

OATMEAL

Plain Oatmeal

The ratio is 2 cups water to 1 cup rolled oats. Heat water to boiling. Stir in oats. Return to a boil, then reduce heat, cover, and simmer a few minutes, stirring occasionally.

Soft rolled oats will make creamier oatmeal.

Sweet Oatmeal

4 cups water	cinnamon
2 cups rolled oats	rice syrup
½ cup raisins or currants	plain or vanilla soymilk and/or
1 peeled apple, grated or chopped	apple juice

1. Stir raisins, apple, and cinnamon into the boiling water along with the oats. When cooked, spoon into bowls and add rice syrup and soymilk.

Rolled Rye, Soy, or Wheat Cereal

Hot cereal can also be made from rye, soy, or wheat flakes. The ratio is 3 cups
water to 1 cup grain and the cooking time is about 10 minutes. Leftovers of
these cooked grains can be served with vegetable dishes for lunch or dinner.

Oat Bran

The ratio is 3 cups of water to 1 cup of oat bran.
1. Combine oat bran and water; mix well.
2. Bring to a boil, then reduce heat and cook about 2 minutes, stirring
   occasionally.
3. You can cook it with raisins or currants, apples, or other fruit, and stir rice
   syrup and soymilk into the pot of cereal or each bowlful.

CornMeal Porridge

3½ cups boiling water	1½ cups cornmeal
	1½ cups cold water

1. Heat 3½ cups of water to boiling in a saucepan.
2. Mix together the cornmeal and cold water and gradually stir into the boiling
   water. Reduce heat, and cook, stirring, a few more minutes.
3. Serve with rice syrup and plain or vanilla soymilk.
4. Unsweetened leftovers can be a dinner grain, with Mexican-type dishes, such
   as bean-vegetable-salsa combinations.

Corn Grits (Hominy)

The ratio is 4 cups of water to 1 cup of grits.
1. Stir grits into boiling water. Reduce heat to medium low, cover, and cook
   5-7 minutes, stirring occasionally, until thickened.
2. You can cook it with raisins or currants or add them to your bowl along with
   rice syrup and plain or vanilla soymilk.
3. Eat it for breakfast, it's porridge. Eat it for dessert, it's pudding. Leftover
   dessert can be breakfast; leftover breakfast can be dessert.

Couscous with Apricots

¾ cup cut-up or processor-chopped dried apricots
1 quart water or apple juice
1 tblsp lemon juice
1⅓ cups couscous

1. Place apricots, water or apple juice, and lemon juice in a pan, cover, and bring to a boil.
2. When liquid boils, add couscous and stir until it boils again.
3. Remove from heat and let sit about 15 minutes, until couscous is soft and all liquid is absorbed.
4. If you like, serve with raisins or currants, soymilk, and rice syrup.

Brown Rice Cream Cereal

You can buy it in a box or make your own. Bake brown rice on a dry baking pan at 350° about 1 hour, until nicely toasted. Stir or shake the rice every 10 minutes or so after the first half hour to prevent overbrowning. Then grind it in a grain mill.

The ratio is 3½ cups of water to 1 cup of dry rice cream. Combine in a pan. Bring to a boil while stirring. Reduce heat to low. Cover and simmer 5 minutes. Remove from heat and stir until smooth.

You can cook it with raisins or currants and cinnamon, or add them to your bowl along with rice syrup and plain or vanilla soymilk.

Plain rice cream, with nothing added, is very soothing to an upset stomach. Of course, if you eat nothing but what's in this book, you may never get an upset stomach, unless you have the flu or if you've just experienced something like an 11-hour (more than double the scheduled time), rough, mass-seasickness ferry crossing from Nova Scotia to Newfoundland. Then you'll be glad you carry rice cream as an adjunct to your first-aid kit. Peppermint tea works wonders, too.

Multi-grain Hot Cereal

Prepare your own combinations of rolled oats, wheat flakes, rye flakes, soy flakes, corn meal, grits, brown rice cream, oat bran, and Wheatena. Include grains left over from yesterday's dinner, such as brown rice, couscous, and millet.

Brown Rice, Couscous, Millet, or Oatmeal Porridge

2 cups cooked brown rice, couscous, or millet (p. 3)
    or 2 cups plain oatmeal (p. 22)
1½-2 cups vanilla soymilk
½ cup raisins
2-4 tblsp rice syrup
½ tsp cinnamon or nutmeg
½-1 cup chopped fresh fruit, such as apples or peaches (optional),
    or canned crushed pineapple
½-1 cup berries (optional)
½ cup crunchy wheat and barley cereal (optional)

Combine grain, soymilk, raisins, rice syrup, cinnamon or nutmeg, and fruit in a
    saucepan. Bring to a boil over medium heat. Simmer about 10 minutes, stirring.
    If using berries and/or cereal, stir in during the last few minutes of cooking.

Multi-grain Porridge

Use any combination of leftover grains along with the other porridge ingredients.

BREADFAST

Cinnamon Toast

1. Toast wholegrain, shortening-free bread slices or bagel halves lightly. Spread
   on rice syrup and sprinkle with cinnamon. Bake or toast in toaster oven or
   place under broiler until bubbly.
2. Or, heat toaster oven to 350°. Spread rice syrup and sprinkle cinnamon on
   bread slices or bagel halves. Then bake until bubbly.

French Toast

1. Preheat oven to 350°.
2. Place slices of wholegrain bread on a nonstick or lightly oiled baking sheet or
   pan. Pour plain or vanilla soymilk (and some orange juice, if you like) over the
   slices. Really soak the bread—it's OK if it doesn't all soak in at first; it will.
   Sprinkle with cinnamon. Depending on the type of bread, the depth of the
   pan, and your preferred softness or crispness, bake 30-60 minutes. For crisper
   French toast, broil for 4-5 minutes on each side, watching closely.
3. Top with rice syrup and/or any fruit topping.

PANCAKES

The basic recipe makes about 12 small (about 2-inch) or 4 large (4-5 inch)
  pancakes. Two batches—the same or different—are about right for two people.

1½ cups flour—some combinations are listed below;
¼ cup soy powder can be mixed with the flour
scant 1½ tsp baking powder
water, orange juice, or other fruit juice
prepared fruit (see below)

All-wheat (or Spelt) Pancakes
1½ cups whole wheat bread flour or spelt flour

Combination Pancakes
½ cup whole wheat bread flour
or spelt flour with 1 cup of any
other ground grain, such as
brown rice flour, buckwheat
flour, cornmeal, oat flour, barley
flour, amaranth flour, soy flour,
or rolled oats

Multi-grain Pancakes
rounded ¼ cup each: whole
wheat bread flour or spelt flour,
brown rice flour, cornmeal,
rolled oats or oat flour, and
buckwheat, barley, or amaranth
flour

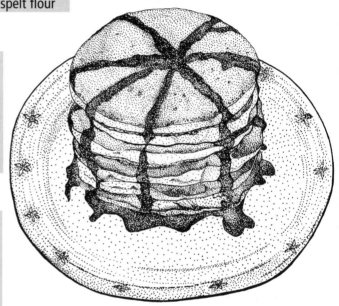

1. Place a nonstick or lightly oiled baking sheet in the oven and preheat to 450°.
2. Combine flours and baking powder. Stir in enough liquid to make a medium-
   thick batter.
3. Spoon onto hot baking sheet. Bake until lightly browned on one side, then flip
   and bake a few more minutes.

Grain-and-Flour Pancakes

For extra-hearty, stick-to-the-ribs pancakes, substitute a cooked whole grain, such as amaranth, barley, brown rice, buckwheat, millet, oats, quinoa, or wheat berries for half the flour. You can omit the baking powder.

Serve small pancakes as a pancake "flower": Arrange pancakes in a circle around the edge of a dinner plate. Have a fruit salad or any combination of fruit ready to fill the flower's center, such as baked apples (p. 205), applesauce or pearsauce (p. 207); chopped apples, pears, peaches, apricots, nectarines, plums, pineapple, kiwifruit, papaya, mango, or bananas; strawberries, blueberries, raspberries, or blackberries. Top pancakes with rice-fruit juice syrup (below), rice syrup (heat for easy pouring), fruit topping (p. 203), or all-fruit jam, and spoon on lots of fruit.

RICE-FRUIT JUICE SYRUP

Combine rice syrup with a small amount of orange juice or other fruit juice, to desired thinness.

POLENTA PANCAKES

1. Prepare cornmeal porridge (p. 23), except cook and stir longer, no less than 20 minutes and as much as an hour. The longer it cooks, the thicker the cooled polenta.
2. Allow polenta to cool (for maximum firmness, chill in the refrigerator), then slice and bake on a nonstick or lightly oiled baking sheet about 10 minutes on each side.

FRUIT 'N' POLENTA PANCAKES

Stir grated apple and/or crushed pineapple—or other grated or mashed fruit—into the cooked polenta before it cools.

CORNMEAL-PUMPKIN PANCAKES

½ cup cornmeal
1 cup boiling water
¾ cup plain or vanilla soymilk
heaping ¼ cup pumpkin or
    winter squash purée (p. 161)
2 ounces tofu, mashed (optional)

1 cup whole wheat or spelt flour
1 tsp baking powder
1 tblsp rice syrup
½ cup crushed pineapple or
    2 grated apples (optional)

1. Place a nonstick or lightly oiled baking sheet in the oven and preheat to 450°.
2. Gradually add the cornmeal to the boiling water while stirring vigorously. Add the soymilk and stir until smooth.
3. Stir in the pumpkin and mashed tofu. Combine flour and baking powder and stir into the cornmeal mixture. Stir in the rice syrup and fruit.
4. Spoon onto hot baking sheet.
5. Bake about 10 minutes on one side, then flip and bake 5-10 more minutes.

This makes about ten 4-inch pancakes.

BREAD

QUICK BREADS

MUFFINS, BISCUITS, AND CRACKERS

IN A CLASS BY ITSELF

YEAST BREADS

Note: Spelt flour can be substituted for whole wheat bread or pastry flour, with excellent results.

QUICK BREADS

SCOTCH SODA BREAD

3 cups rolled oats
2 cups water
3 cups whole wheat bread flour
2 tblsp rice syrup
2 tsp baking soda
¾ tsp baking powder

1. Preheat oven to 350°.
2. Combine oats, flour, baking soda, and baking powder. Add water and rice syrup. Mix well.
3. Shape into one large or two small round loaves. Place on a nonstick or lightly oiled baking sheet. Cut 2 short parallel slashes in the dough about ½ inch deep.
4. Bake 45-50 minutes.

IRISH SODA BREAD

2 cups whole wheat bread flour
1 tsp baking soda
1 tblsp rice syrup
1 cup plain soymilk or soy yogurt (p. 10) or
   2 tblsp soy powder and 1 cup water

1. Preheat oven to 375°.
2. Combine the flour and baking soda. If you're using soy powder, add it now. Add rice syrup and soymilk, yogurt, or water. Dough should be neither sticky nor too dry.
3. Knead about 5 minutes, then shape into a rounded loaf. Cut 2 short parallel slashes in the dough about ½ inch deep. Place on a nonstick or lightly oiled baking sheet.
4. Bake 25-30 minutes, until well browned.

QUICK RAISIN BREAD

2 cups whole wheat flour
½ cup vanilla soymilk
1 cup raisins
½ cup orange juice
1 tsp baking soda
2 tblsp rice syrup
2 tblsp hot water

1. Preheat oven to 350°.
2. Mix together the flour, raisins, and baking soda.
3. Add the rest and mix well. Place in a nonstick or lightly oiled 8- by 4-inch loaf pan.
4. Bake about 40 minutes, until a toothpick inserted in the center comes out clean. Remove from pan.

This is great lightly toasted, spread with rice syrup, sprinkled with cinnamon, and then retoasted until bubbly under the broiler or in a toaster oven.

FLATBREAD

Brown Rice Flatbread

2 cups brown rice flour
2 cups whole wheat pastry flour
2+ cups water

Brown Rice and Cornmeal Flatbread

1⅓ cups brown rice flour
1⅓ cups whole wheat pastry flour
1⅓ cups cornmeal
2+ cups water

1. Preheat oven to 400°.
2. Combine flours. Add water until consistency of batter. Pour onto a nonstick or lightly oiled 12- by 14- inch baking pan.
3. Bake 20 minutes, then flip the whole thing over and bake 20 more minutes.
Great spread with apple cider jelly.

Berry Flatbread

1. Add 1 cup fresh blueberries or blackberries to the batter.

Great with rice syrup.

Oatcakes

3 cups soft rolled oats
3 cups water
3 cups whole wheat pastry flour
2 tblsp rice syrup

1. Preheat oven to 350°.
2. Combine oats and flour. Stir in water. Add rice syrup; stir well.
   Add more water if needed for a batter consistency.
3. Transfer to a nonstick or lightly oiled 12- by 14-inch baking pan.
   Fill the pan evenly.
4. Bake 20 minutes, then flip the whole thing over and bake 20 more minutes.
   Cool slightly and cut into squares or rectangles.

Steamed Brown Bread

1 cup whole wheat bread flour
2 cups soymilk*
1 cup rye or buckwheat flour
½ cup barley malt syrup or rice syrup
1 cup cornmeal
½ cup raisins or currants
2 tsp baking soda

1. In a fairly deep pot with a tight-fitting lid, heat several inches of water to
   boiling.
2. Combine the flours, cornmeal, and soda. Stir in the soymilk and syrup,
   then the raisins.
3. Pour into four lightly oiled 15-oz cans. The cans should be just over half full.
   Cap cans with tin foil, place upright in the hot water, and simmer 2 hours.
   The water should be about halfway up the cans.
4. Remove from pot, and when cool enough to handle, slide breads from cans.

*Or, mix ½ cup soy powder with the dry ingredients, and use 2 cups water

MUFFINS, BISCUITS, AND CRACKERS

CORNMEAL MUFFINS:

about 12

1½ cups cornmeal
½ cup whole wheat pastry flour
1½ tsp baking powder
1½ cups plain or vanilla soymilk or orange juice, or combination
2 tblsp rice syrup or barley malt syrup
blueberries or blackberries (optional)

1. Preheat oven to 400°.
2. Combine cornmeal, flour, and baking powder.
3. Add soymilk and/or orange juice, rice syrup, and berries. Stir just enough to moisten.
4. Fill nonstick or lightly oiled muffin tins ⅔ full.
5. Bake 25-30 minutes.

BUCKWHEAT-CORNMEAL MUFFINS:

about 12

1 cup buckwheat flour
1¼ cups plain or vanilla soymilk
½ cup cornmeal
2 tblsp rice syrup
1 tsp baking powder

1. Preheat oven to 400°.
2. Combine buckwheat flour, cornmeal, and baking powder.
3. Add soymilk and rice syrup. Stir just enough to moisten.
4. Fill nonstick or lightly oiled muffin tins ⅔ full.
5. Bake 15-20 minutes.

Carrot Muffins (or Cake)

about 24 muffins

2 cups whole wheat pastry flour
1½ tsp baking soda
2 tsp cinnamon
½-1 cup raisins
2 cups grated carrots
¾ cup total orange juice and/or vanilla soymilk
¼ cup rice syrup
2 tsp vanilla
½ cup crushed pineapple, applesauce, or grated raw apple (optional)

1. Preheat oven to 325°.
2. Combine flour, soda, cinnamon, and raisins in a large bowl. Be sure the raisins are un-clumped. In another bowl, combine the remaining ingredients. Stir wet into dry.
3. Fill nonstick or lightly oiled muffin tins about ⅔ full.
4. Bake about 45 minutes.

Or, make one dozen muffins and one 9-inch round carrot cake.

Rhubarb Muffins

Replace one cup of whole wheat flour with cornmeal, omit raisins, and substitute 2 cups chopped rhubarb for the grated carrots.

PUMPKIN-DATE MUFFINS

about 12

1½ cups whole wheat pastry flour
½ cup dates
1½ tsp baking powder
⅔ cup plain or vanilla soymilk
½ tsp nutmeg
½ cup pumpkin purée (p. 161)
½ tsp cinnamon
¼-½ cup rice syrup

1. Preheat oven to 400°.
2. Combine flour, baking powder, nutmeg, and cinnamon. Stir in dates.
3. Separately, mix soymilk, pumpkin, and rice syrup.
4. Add to flour mixture and stir just until dry ingredients are moistened.
5. Fill nonstick or lightly oiled muffin tins about ⅔ full.
6. Bake 20-25 minutes.

QUICK SOY BISCUITS

about 12

1 cup whole wheat flour
⅔ cup orange juice
¾ cup soy grits or granules
1-2 tblsp rice syrup
1½ tsp baking powder
½ tsp lemon juice
¼ tsp cinnamon
¼ tsp vanilla

1. Preheat oven to 325°.
2. Combine dry ingredients. Combine wet ingredients separately.
3. Stir wet into dry.
4. Drop by spoonfuls onto a nonstick or lightly oiled baking sheet.
5. Bake about 20 minutes.

optional additions:

Stir in berries, raisins, currants, or chopped dried fruit.

BROWN RICE BISCUITS

1 cup brown rice flour
about ¾ cup water
1 cup whole wheat pastry flour
raisins or currants (optional)

1. Combine ingredients with enough water to make a fairly thick batter. Let batter sit ½ hour.
2. Flatten on a cutting board, then cut into biscuit rounds with the rim of a cup or glass, and place on a nonstick or lightly oiled baking sheet. Or just drop by tablespoons onto the baking sheet.
3. Bake at 325°. Flip after 10-15 minutes, when bottom is golden brown, and continue baking another 10-15 minutes.

CINNAMON BISCUITS

2 cups whole wheat bread flour
¼ cup rice syrup
½ tsp baking soda
1/4 cup plain or vanilla soymilk
1½ tsp baking powder
¼-½ cup water
1¼ tsp cinnamon

1. Preheat oven to 425°.
2. Combine dry ingredients in a bowl. Separately, mix the rice syrup, soymilk, and ¼ cup water.
3. Add to flour mixture and stir just until moistened, adding water if necessary.
4. Drop the dough in mounds on a nonstick or lightly oiled baking sheet.
5. Bake at 400° for 10 minutes, then lower heat to 350° and bake 8-10 more minutes, until biscuits are golden.

QUICK YEAST BISCUITS

2 tblsp yeast
2 tblsp sesame oil
2 cups lukewarm water
about 4½ cups whole wheat bread flour
2 tblsp rice syrup

1. Mix and knead. Let rise 15 minutes or until double.
2. Press thin, then cut into about 16 rounds with the rim of a cup or glass.
3. Transfer to a nonstick or lightly oiled baking pan.
4. Bake at 350° for 10-15 minutes.

Pretzels

1. Prepare dough for Quick Yeast Biscuits.
2. Roll into ropes, then form into traditional pretzel shapes, or any shape you like.

JOHNNYCAKES

2 cups cornmeal
about 2½ cups boiling water

1. Preheat oven to 400°.
2. Pour the boiling water over the cornmeal and mix thoroughly to form a thick
   batter. Shape into round or oval cakes about ½ inch thick.
3. Place on a nonstick or lightly oiled baking sheet.
4. Bake 10-15 minutes on each side.

Oatmeal Crackers

2½ cups soft rolled oats
½ cup cold water

1. Preheat oven to 275°.
2. Stir 2 cups of oats together with the water in a bowl until the dough holds together in a mass.
3. Sprinkle a work surface with ¼ cup oats and place dough on top. Use a rolling pin to roll dough to ⅛-inch thickness. To avoid sticking, move and lift dough as you roll it out, and sprinkle it with more oats. If cracks form, seal them with your fingers. Trim to form a rectangle, about 10 inches by 7 inches.
4. Lift dough halves with a spatula and place on an ungreased baking sheet. Score dough with a knife (don't cut through) into 1½-inch squares.
5. Bake 30 minutes, turn over, and bake 15-20 minute more. Curled edges can be prevented by occasionally pressing them down with a spatula while baking.
6. Remove from oven, cool, and break into squares.

IN A CLASS BY ITSELF

Brown Rice Bread

1 large or 2 small loaves

4 cups cooked brown rice
1 tblsp tamari
4+ cups whole wheat bread flour
hot water

1. In a large bowl, combine brown rice and flour. Mix with a fork until all rice grains are separated and coated with flour. Add tamari and enough hot water to make a moist but not wet dough. Knead 15 minutes, adding more flour if it's too sticky. Kneading with one hand right in the bowl works fine.
2. Form into one or two rounds or two loaves. Oil the dough, place on a nonstick or lightly oiled baking sheet or pie pans, or in loaf pans, cover with a damp towel, and let sit 8-12 hours.
3. Bake at 325° about one hour.

YEAST BREADS

A good loaf of store-bought bread is hard to find: impossible in many supermarkets and not guaranteed in coops or natural food stores, where prices of $3-$5 per loaf are not uncommon. You can often find faultless whole wheat pita in supermarkets, usually near the deli section. But in the bread aisle, or even the fresh-baked section, once you eliminate those not made of wholegrain flour, you drastically reduce the possibilities. A quick, gentle squeeze will tell all—if it compresses, go on to the next. Or, scrutinize each loaf's ingredients list and eliminate those containing shortening, sweetener, dough conditioner, preservatives, or other unwelcome additives. By then you'll be glad you know all about.....

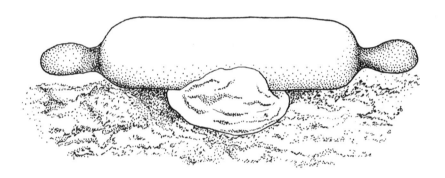

YEAST BREAD BASICS

Because of the properties of yeast, temperature is crucial to success. Yeast is a living plant that feeds on sweeteners and the natural sugar in dough. Yeast multiplies and emits carbon dioxide bubbles. These bubbles are held in place by gluten, the stretchy stuff that forms in kneaded dough and creates a network of tunnels or rubbery balloons that trap the gas and allow the bread to rise. "Baby-bottle" temperature, slightly warm—test with your wrist, is optimal for the yeast to feed and rise. If the ingredients or rising temperature are too hot, the yeast will be killed. If they're too cold, the yeast remains inactive. So, have the ingredients at room temperature, or even warm the flour a little bit.

Use stoneground whole wheat bread flour. It's the heartiest and healthiest, because the wheat germ and bran, which contain a wealth of important nutrients, are intact. Stoneground flour retains B vitamins (for a healthy nervous system) and vitamin E (an antioxidant) which are destroyed by the high heat of steel roller milling. Also, stoneground flour is less likely to get rancid, because the germ doesn't get flaked into an oily mass.

Kneading is repeated folding, pushing, and turning of the dough. The dough should be just dry enough that it doesn't stick to the breadboard. If you add too much flour, the yeast can't handle the extra work, and the bread won't rise as well.

The dough rises twice, once all together in a large oiled bowl, and once in its bread pans after you've formed it into loaves. Always keep it covered (with a light dishtowel, for example) while rising.

Be inventive about finding a warm place for rising. The commonest place is in the oven. Warm it first, then shut it off and put the bowl or breadpans in. Reheat it every 20 minutes or so. REMEMBER TO TURN THE OVEN OFF OR ALL IS LOST!! Or place a pan of hot water on the oven floor and set bowl or pans above. If you're using the oven for something else, place the bowl and bread pans on the stovetop. You can also place them in a sunny spot behind a south-facing window, behind a wood stove or near a radiator (turn frequently), or on a towel on a heating pad set to medium.
If you have an oil burner, its top is a good spot; if you have radiant-heated floors, you're also all set. Be sure there's no draft. It could break the gluten and cause the dough to fall.

Recipes often say, "Let rise until double in bulk" for the first rising, in the bowl. Push your finger gently into the dough about half an inch. If the dough stays put when you remove your finger, it's ready. It should be light and airy, so that when you "punch it down" (press your fist down into it), your fist sinks right through. For the second rising, in the pans, it's ready when it looks like a loaf of bread!

When you're ready to bake, it's important to preheat the oven completely, so the yeast is killed right away. Otherwise, it will go berserk, the dough will overreach, and then the loaves will collapse. Keep the breadpans separated and away from the oven sides, to allow the heat to circulate. Convection ovens are good for baking bread.

The finished loaf should be a rich, deep color, but not too dark. When you tap its bottom, it should sound and feel hollow. Otherwise, it may be underdone— too moist inside. And the loaf should fall right out the pan when turned upside down. Place it right across the pan-top or on a rack to cool. It slices best with a long, firm, sharp, serrated knife.

WHOLE WHEAT BREAD

2 loaves

4½ cups whole wheat bread flour	2 tblsp applesauce (p. 207)
2 cups lukewarm water	1½ tblsp yeast
1 tsp salt	1 tblsp rice syrup or barley malt syrup

1. Combine flour, salt, and yeast in a large bowl. Stir well. Stir in water, applesauce, and rice syrup.
2. Turn out on floured board and knead 10 minutes. Place in lightly oiled bowl, turning to coat the whole dough. Cover with a towel and let rise in a warm place ½ hour or more until doubled.
3. Cut in half and let rest 5-10 minutes. Form into loaves and put in nonstick or lightly oiled bread pans. Cover and let rise until above tops of pans.
4. Bake at 350° for 30 minutes.

CINNAMON-RAISIN BREAD

1. After the first rising, roll out one or both loaves to a large rectangle.
2. Spread with rice syrup and sprinkle with raisins and cinnamon.
3. Roll up and tuck ends under.
4. Place in pans, cover, let rise, and bake, as above.

OATMEAL BREAD

2 loaves

1½ cups boiling water	1 tblsp yeast
1 cup rolled oats	2 cups lukewarm water
½ cup rice syrup or barley malt syrup	about 8 cups whole wheat bread flour

1. Pour the boiling water over the oats and let stand 30 minutes.
2. Add rice syrup. Dissolve yeast in the warm water and add to the oat mixture.
3. Beat, and work in enough flour to make a medium-soft dough.
4. Turn onto a floured board and knead until smooth, about 10 minutes.
5. Place in a clean, oiled bowl and turn to oil the top. Cover and let rise until doubled, about 1 hour.
6. Divide and shape the dough into 2 loaves and place in nonstick or lightly oiled bread pans. Cover and let rise in a warm place until doubled, about 45 minutes.
7. Preheat the oven to 400°.
8. Bake 5 minutes, then lower the heat to 350° and bake about 40 more minutes.

Raisin Pumpernickel

2 loaves

2¼ cups cold water	1 cup raisins
2½ -3 cups whole wheat bread flour	2 tblsp yeast
¾ cup cornmeal	¼ cup lukewarm water
2½ -3 cups rye flour	2 tsp rice syrup
¼ cup barley malt syrup	

1. Stir the cold water into the cornmeal in a saucepan and heat, stirring, over medium heat until the mixture boils and thickens. Remove from heat and stir in malt syrup. Cool to lukewarm.
2. Sprinkle yeast over the warm water and stir. Add rice syrup and let stand in a warm place 10 minutes.
3. Add the yeast mixture to the cornmeal. Stir in 2 cups each whole wheat and rye flour to form a soft dough.
4. Turn onto a floured board. Knead the dough, adding enough of the remaining flours to make a non-sticky dough. Knead 10 minutes, until very smooth.
5. Knead in the raisins. Place in a clean oiled bowl and turn to oil the top. Cover and let rise in a warm place until doubled, about 1 hour.
6. Punch down and divide in half. Shape each half into a well-rounded loaf and put on a nonstick or lightly oiled baking sheet or pie pan dusted with cornmeal.
7. Cover and let rise until doubled, about 45 minutes.
8. Preheat the oven to 375°. Bake 30-40 minutes, or until done.

English Muffin Bread

2 loaves

2 tblsp yeast	5-6 cups whole wheat bread flour
2 tblsp rice syrup or barley malt syrup	2 tsp salt
½ + 2 cups lukewarm water	cornmeal

1. Soften yeast with rice syrup in ½ cup of the lukewarm water.
2. Dissolve salt in the rest of the water. Add yeast mixture and one cup flour. Beat well. Add the rest of the flour.
3. Knead briefly on a floured board. Place in a clean oiled bowl; turn to oil the whole dough. Cover and let rise in a warm place until double.
4. Punch down, divide in half. Shape into regular or round loaves.
5. Sprinkle nonstick or lightly oiled loaf pans (or a baking sheet or two round baking pans or pie tins) with cornmeal.
6. Place loaves in pans and sprinkle with more cornmeal. Let rise.
7. Bake in 375° oven for 25-35 minutes.

OLD-FASHIONED RYE BREAD

2 loaves

6 tblsp cornmeal
1½ cups rye flour
½ cup cold water
2½ cups whole wheat bread flour
1 cup boiling water
1 cup soft, smooth mashed potatoes
1 tsp salt2 tblsp caraway seeds
1 tsp rice syrup or barley malt syrup
¼ cup warm water
3 tblsp yeast

1. Mix the cornmeal with the cold water in a small saucepan. Add the boiling water and cook 2 minutes, stirring constantly. Remove from heat, add salt, and let cool until lukewarm.
2. In a cup or small bowl, dissolve rice syrup or barley malt syrup in the warm water, then stir in yeast and wait for a nice head of foam.
3. Combine flours, cornmeal mixture, mashed potatoes, caraway seeds, and yeast mixture in a bowl.
4. Knead to a stiff but slightly sticky dough.
5. Place in an oiled bowl, turn to oil the whole dough, cover, and let rise in a warm place until double.
6. Punch down and form into 2 loaves. Place in nonstick or lightly oiled bread pans.
7. *Or*, form into round loaves and place on pie tins or a baking sheet.
8. Cover and let rise until doubled.
9. Preheat oven to 375°. Bake about 45 minutes.

LIGHTER RYE BREAD: LESS RYE, MORE RISING

1 loaf

1½ tsp yeast
½ tsp salt
1½ cups warm water
1 tblsp oil
¼ cup rice syrup
1½ tsp total caraway seeds, whole and/or ground
3-3½ cups whole wheat bread flour
1 cup rye flour

1. Dissolve yeast in water and stir in rice syrup. Let sit about 5 minutes, then add 2 cups flour. Beat well to form a smooth, thick, elastic batter. Let sit about 1 hour, until light and foamy. Stir in salt, oil, and caraway, then rye flour and more bread flour. Knead about 10 minutes, adding more bread flour as needed until the dough is smooth and elastic.
2. Let rise 45 to 60 minutes. Punch down, knead a few minutes, and let rise another 45 to 60 minutes.
3. Form into a loaf, place in a nonstick or lightly oiled bread pan, and let rise about 45 minutes, until almost doubled in bulk.
4. Preheat oven to 350°. Bake about an hour, remove from pan, and cool before slicing.

PITA (POCKET BREAD)

6 pitas

2 cups lukewarm water
1 tblsp rice syrup or barley malt syrup
5+ cups whole wheat bread flour
1 tblsp yeast
1 tsp salt

1. Stir the rice syrup into the water. In a large bowl, thoroughly mix 2 cups flour, yeast, and salt. Gradually stir in liquid. Continue adding flour and mixing until the dough is soft. Knead 8-10 minutes.
2. Place in a lightly oiled bowl, turn to coat with oil, cover, and let rise 1 hour. Punch down and turn onto a lightly floured board. Cover and let rest 30 minutes.
3. Place a baking sheet in the oven and heat to 450°.
4. Divide dough into 6 equal parts. Shape each into a ball. Use a rolling pin or a jar on a lightly floured surface to roll each ball into an 8-inch circle. (Roll from the center outward to form even circles.) As each is rolled, set it aside on a lightly floured surface.
5. Then, use a flipper to slide the pitas onto the hot baking sheet and place on the lowest oven rack. Bake 5 minutes. When they're puffed up beautifully and lightly browned, they're done.

BAGELS

about 12

1½ cups lukewarm water
3 tblsp rice syrup or barley malt syrup
1 tblsp yeast
about 5 cups whole wheat bread flour

1. In a large bowl, dissolve 2 tblsp rice syrup in the warm water. Sprinkle the yeast over and stir to dissolve. Add flour gradually, until the dough is quite firm and leaves sides of bowl. Knead 10 minutes. Let rise in an oiled bowl until doubled; this may take up to 2 hours.
2. Punch down and knead until smooth and elastic. Pinch off pieces of dough and form into bagel shapes. Let rise 15 more minutes.
3. Meanwhile heat 1 quart water to boiling and stir in 1 tblsp rice syrup. Drop in bagels and let boil about five minutes on each side. Move them if necessary to make sure they float to the top.
4. Remove from water, let dry 5 minutes, then place on nonstick or lightly oiled baking sheet.
5. Bake at 375° for 10-15 minutes on each side.

Soups

LIGHTER SOUPS

COLD SOUPS

DINNER SOUPS

LIGHTER SOUPS

INSTANT MISO SOUP

1. Place 1 heaping tablespoon of miso in a mug. Add a small amount of boiling water and stir to dissolve.
2. Fill with boiling water and stir. You can press a clove of garlic and stir it in. This is both delicious and medicinal.

Other additions: Place hot cooked pasta, rice, or other grain in a bowl and pour the soup over. Top with sprouts.

MISO SOUP WITH VEGETABLES

fresh vegetables (see below)
boiling water and/or stock
medium or dark miso: 1 heaping tblsp per cup of water
optional: cubed tofu
        warm cooked brown rice
        sprouts, such as mung, alfalfa, or red clover
        diced cabbage, chives, and/or parsley

1. In a small amount of water or stock, sauté diced fresh vegetables, such as onions, bell peppers, broccoli and cauliflower florets and stems, celery, carrots, summer squash, garlic, kale, mushrooms, kohlrabi, green beans, turnips, rutabaga, parsnips, edible pod peas, sea vegetables.
2. Use 2-4 times as much water and/or stock as diced raw vegetables.
3. Add boiling liquid and cubed tofu to the sautéed vegetables.
4. Add miso thinned in a little of the hot liquid. If using spinach, tear leaves and add now and cook 1 more minute.
5. To serve, put brown rice in bowls and pour soup over.
6. Garnish with sprouts and/or diced cabbage, chives, and/or parsley.

PARSLEY AND/OR KALE SOUP

2 or more cloves garlic, pressed or finely chopped
large bunch parsley and/or kale, rinsed and chopped
6-8 cups total water and/or stock
optional garnishes: tamari, tiny tofu cubes, hot sauce, chives

1. Sauté garlic briefly in a small amount of water, then add wet greens and steam until bright green. Add liquid and boil.
2. Lower heat and cook about 5 minutes, until soft. Serve hot; add garnishes.

GARLIC SOUP

8-10 cloves garlic, pressed or finely chopped
4-6 cups water
2 tblsp tamari or 1-1½ tblsp miso
2 tblsp chopped fresh, or 1 tblsp dried, parsley

1. Sauté garlic in a small amount of water for 2-3 minutes, just until soft.
2. Add water, cover, and bring to a boil. Reduce heat and simmer about 15 minutes.
3. Add tamari or miso thinned in some of the hot broth.
4. Ladle into bowls and top with a small amount of parsley.

RAMEN

Ramen is a "convenience" soup, a package of dried broth mix and noodles so thin they cook in 3 minutes. Buy coop or natural foods store ramen, with wholegrain noodles that were steamed, not fried.

You can augment the mix with diced or chopped fresh vegetables and more real miso (thinned in a small amount of hot water), and garnish with sprouts. Remember to break up the noodles or you'll be dealing with meter-long cooked noodles.

ONION-TOMATO SOUP

1 quart thinly sliced onions
2 quarts total water (with 2 tblsp vegetable broth powder, optional) and/or stock
1 cup cubed peeled turnip or rutabaga
½ cup total tomato sauce and/or salsa
freshly ground black pepper

1. Sauté onions in a small amount of water in a large pot. Add water or stock, turnips, tomato sauce/salsa, and pepper.
2. Cover, bring to a boil, then reduce heat and simmer 45 minutes.

Onion Soup with Tamari

5 cups sliced onions
fresh ginger, cut into 2 tblsp tiny sticks (or ½ tsp ground dried ginger)
7½ cups water
2 or more cloves garlic, pressed or finely chopped
1 tsp each fresh, or ½ tsp each dried, oregano, thyme, and sage
2-4 tblsp snipped or crumbled sea vegetables (optional)
½ cup tamari
freshly ground black pepper

1. Sauté onions and ginger in a small amount of water in a large pot.
2. When slightly brown, add the rest of the ingredients.
3. Cover, bring to a boil, and simmer several minutes.

Hot and Sour Tofu Soup

4 cups total water (with 1 tblsp vegetable broth powder, optional) and/or stock
6 dried mushrooms
2 tblsp snipped or crumbled sea vegetables
6 oz tofu, pressed (p. 6) and cubed
marinade for tofu: 2 tblsp tamari, 1 tblsp mirin, 1 tblsp brown rice vinegar
2 cups total chopped or sliced Chinese cabbage, green cabbage, and/or celery
1 cup sliced onions
1 tsp grated fresh ginger, or ¼ tsp dried ginger
2 tblsp vinegar
½ tsp (more or less) hot sauce, hot pepper flakes, chili powder, or white pepper

1. Boil 1 cup water or stock and pour oven mushrooms and sea vegetables in a small bowl. Soak 15 minutes. Put remaining water or stock in a soup pot.
2. Place tofu cubes in marinade.
3. Drain mushrooms and sea vegetables, adding the liquid to the soup pot. Shred the mushrooms and add to the liquid. Bring to a boil, reduce heat, and simmer 5 minutes.
4. Add tofu, marinade, vegetables, and ginger, and simmer 2-3 more minutes.
5. Remove from heat and stir in vinegar and hot sauce or pepper.

Carrot-Only Soup

Using a juicer, prepare carrot juice (p. 216), or buy some at a coop or natural foods store. Then heat the juice in a pan— just until warm, to retain the enzymes.

PUMPKIN SOUP

½ cup soy powder
3 cups total water and/or stock from steaming pumpkin
2 cups pumpkin purée (p. 161)
1 tsp rice syrup
¼ tsp ground nutmeg
⅛ tsp ground white pepper
toasted bread slices
tiny cubes of tofu

1. Measure soy powder into pot and stir in the water or stock. Heat slowly until hot.
2. Add pumpkin, rice syrup, pepper, and nutmeg. Heat through, then simmer gently 3-4 minutes.
3. Serve with toast slice and tofu cubes floating on top.

Instead of pumpkin, you can use puréed winter squash.

Pumpkin-Vegetable-Grain Soup

To transform to a substantial dinner soup, first steam-fry sliced or chunked vegetables, such as carrots, onions, and celery. Then add the other soup ingredients. In place of the toast garnish, stir in a cooked grain.

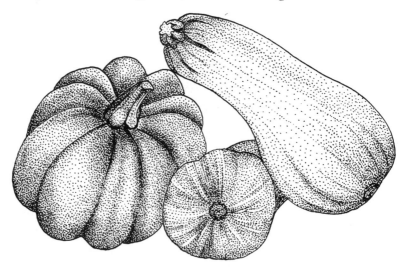

COLD SOUPS

BORSCHT (BEET SOUP)

beets	Egyptian onions (optional)
potatoes	beet tops (optional)
onions	soy yogurt (p. 10) (optional)

1. Peel and dice the beets into ½-inch cubes. Or, dice half of them, and shred, grate, or finely chop the rest. Peel and dice potatoes into ½-inch cubes, or use tiny whole potatoes.
2. Slice the onions very thinly. (Leave Egyptian onions whole.) Place everything in a pot with enough water to make a thin broth.
3. Cover, bring to a boil, reduce heat, and simmer until vegetables are tender. Add chopped beet tops partway through cooking.
4. Stir in soy yogurt when ready to serve. Or, chill the borscht and eat it cold, plain or with soy yogurt.

CHUNKY OR SMOOTH GAZPACHO

2-4 cloves garlic
3 cups chunked tomatoes
1 cup chunked cucumber
½ cup chunked bell pepper
½ cup chunked onion
¼ cup total red wine vinegar and/or lemon juice
2 cups tomato juice (or reconstituted tomato paste)
1 tblsp fresh, or ½ tsp dried, basil
½ tsp each dill weed and dill seed
freshly ground black pepper

1. If using a processor, drop in garlic with the metal blade spinning to mince. Then add the chunks of tomato, cucumber, bell pepper, and onion, and pulse-chop or totally purée, depending on your preferred gazpacho texture. Transfer to a bowl and stir in remaining ingredients.
2. Or, press or finely chop the garlic, finely chop the other vegetables, and combine all ingredients.
3. Either way, chill well and serve with hot sauce, or heat and serve over pasta!

Note: You can use other vegetables, such as broccoli, cabbage, carrots, cauliflower, celery, mushrooms, parsley, and summer squash, in place of or in addition to the cucumber and bell pepper.

CREAMED AND CURRIED SUMMER (OR WINTER) SQUASH SOUP

1½ cups chopped onion
2 tblsp curry
2 tsp grated fresh, or ¾ tsp dried, ginger
5 cups chunked yellow crookneck squash*
4 cups total water (with 1 tblsp vegetable broth powder, optional) and/or stock
½ cup plain soymilk or soy yogurt (p. 10), 1 tblsp soy powder, or 4-6 oz tofu
chopped fresh coriander leaf (optional)

1. Water—sauté the onion. Stir in curry and ginger. Add squash and 2 cups water or stock. Bring to a boil, then reduce heat, cover, and simmer 20 minutes.
2. Purée in a blender or food processor with the soymilk, soy yogurt, soy powder, or tofu. Return to pot, add remaining water, and stir.
3. Reheat or chill and serve cold. Garnish with chopped fresh coriander leaf.

Partly steamed (for easier peeling), peeled, and chunked winter squash can be substituted. Serve hot.

COOL CUCUMBER SOUP

1. Finely chop garlic in a processor. Purée with chopped peeled cucumbers and fresh or dried dill.
2. Thin with soy yogurt (p. 10) and season with freshly ground black pepper.
3. You can also add chopped chives and other herbs such as basil and tarragon.

FRUIT SOUP

½ pound (about 2 cups) mixed dried fruit, such as prunes, apricots, raisins, pears, peaches, or apples
2½ quarts water
2 pounds (about 4 cups) mixed fresh fruit, such as cubed or
  sliced peaches, apricots, pears, plums, or apples, or
  whole strawberries, blueberries, or blackberries
½ cup lemon juice
rice syrup

1. Combine the dried fruits and water in a large saucepan. Bring to a boil and simmer over low heat until tender, about 30 minutes.
2. Add the fresh fruit, except the berries, and cook 5 minutes. Add berries and cook 5 more minutes. Remove from heat and add the lemon juice. Cool and chill. Serve cold or reheat.

DINNER SOUPS

just add wholegrain bread, muffins, biscuits, or crackers.

TOMATO SOUP

½ cup chopped onion
1 cup chopped celery
1 cup total sliced mushrooms, sliced cabbage,
    and/or stems from broccoli or cauliflower (optional)
1-2 carrots, diced or grated
about 1 quart chopped fresh tomatoes
1 tsp each dried (or 2 tsp fresh) basil, marjoram, oregano, and/or parsley
1 quart total hot water and/or stock
freshly ground black pepper and/or hot sauce

1. Sauté the onions, celery, and carrots in a small amount of water until soft.
   Add tomatoes and herbs and simmer gently for 15 minutes.
   If you want a smooth texture, purée this mixture in a food processor.
2. Add the hot liquid, bring the soup to a boil, and simmer on low heat for 5 minutes.
   Season with pepper and/or hot sauce.

For a thicker soup, use less stock and reduce seasonings.
For a creamy soup, blend ¼ cup soy powder or 4 oz tofu with the tomato mixture.
For a heartier soup, add a cup of cooked brown rice.

CARROT SOUP

3 cups thinly sliced carrots
1 cup chopped onion
⅔ cup chopped celery (and/or cabbage and broccoli or cauliflower stems)
1½ cups diced peeled potato
1-2 cloves garlic, pressed or finely chopped
herbs, such as ½ tsp each basil, rosemary, tarragon, thyme, and celery seed
freshly ground black pepper
4 cups total water (with 1 tblsp vegetable broth powder, optional) and/or stock

1. Steam carrots, onion, celery, potato, and garlic in a small amount of water
   for about 10 minutes. Keep the pot covered, but stir occasionally.
2. Add the herbs, pepper, and water or stock. Cover, bring to a boil, reduce heat,
   and simmer about 20 minutes.
3. If you prefer a smooth soup, purée it in batches in a blender or food processor,
   then reheat.
4. Serve with miso or tamari, or hot sauce.

CORN AND CARROT CHOWDER *

1 cup chopped onions or scallions
1 cup peeled, diced potatoes
2 cups diced carrots
2 cups corn kernels
½ cup chopped celery or red pepper (optional)
1 tblsp rice syrup
2 tblsp finely chopped fresh, or 2 tsp dried, parsley
ginger: 1 tblsp grated fresh or ¾ tsp dried
    or dill weed: 1 tblsp chopped fresh or 1 tsp dried
freshly ground black pepper
½ cup soy powder
4 cups total water (with 2 tblsp vegetable broth powder, optional) and/or stock

1. Sauté onions or scallions in a small amount of water until soft.
2. Add remaining vegetables and just enough water to steam them.
    Cover and cook over medium heat 15 minutes.
3. Blend in rice syrup, ginger or dill, pepper, and soy powder.
4. Stir in the water, bring to a boil, and simmer 15 more minutes.
*This is a good use for older, not-in-prime-season, or frozen corn.
    Save the wonderful sweet fresh ears for corn on the cob.*

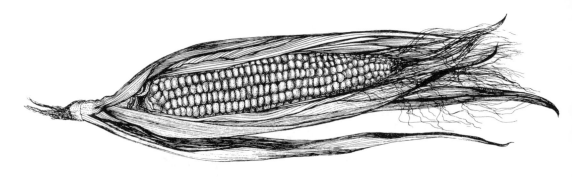

SMOOTH CARROT SOUP

1. Omit the corn, celery or red pepper, parsley, and dill.
2. Sauté onions and steam with potatoes and carrots until they are tender.
3. Add rice syrup, ginger, pepper, and soymilk.
4. Purée. Return to pot and stir in water. Heat through.

Vegetable Soup with Miso

8 cups total water (with 2 tblsp vegetable broth mix, optional) and/or stock
1½ cups sliced or chopped onion
6 large cloves garlic, pressed or finely chopped
one 1-in piece fresh ginger root, peeled and grated or finely chopped
2 cups thinly sliced carrots
1 cup sliced mushrooms
2 cups chopped Chinese cabbage, bok choy, or celery
8 oz tofu, sliced, pressed (p. 6), and cut into small cubes
cayenne or freshly ground black pepper
½ cup miso
chopped fresh parsley

1. Heat the water and/or stock in a large pot. Meanwhile, sauté the onions, garlic, and ginger in a small amount of water for a few minutes, then add the carrots, and finally the mushrooms and Chinese cabbage, bok choy, or celery.
2. Transfer to the heated water and add the tofu and cayenne or pepper. Just before serving, thin miso with some of the hot broth and add to the soup along with the parsley.

"Cream" of Cauliflower Soup

8 cups total water (with 2 tblsp vegetable broth mix, optional) and/or stock
1 cup chopped onion
1 cup grated carrot
1 cup other diced vegetables, such as celery, parsnip, mushrooms, and/or broccoli and cauliflower stems
1 head cauliflower (Break into flowerets and slice the upper part of the stems.)
2 tblsp chopped fresh, or 2 tsp dried, parsley
4-6 oz tofu or ½ cup soy powder (see below)
1 tsp tarragon
1 bay leaf
2 tblsp snipped or crumbled sea vegetables (optional)
freshly ground black pepper

1. In a large pot, use a small amount of the total water or stock to sauté the onion until soft.
2. Add the carrot and diced vegetables and sauté a few more minutes.
3. Add an additional cup of the water or stock along with the cauliflower and half the parsley. Cover and simmer 15 minutes, stirring occasionally.
4. Meanwhile, if you're using tofu, purée it with about 2 more cups of the water (and broth mix) in a blender or processor.
5. Add to soup along with remaining water and seasonings.
   (If you're using soy powder, no need to purée; just stir it in now.)
6. Bring to a boil, then reduce heat and simmer gently for 15-20 minutes.
7. Garnish with remaining parsley.

Potato Chowder

½ cup thinly sliced or chopped onion
½ cup chopped celery (and/or cabbage and broccoli or cauliflower stems)
5 cups total water (with 1 tblsp vegetable broth powder, optional) and/or stock
4 cups peeled and diced potatoes
1 cup finely diced carrots
2 tblsp snipped or crumbled sea vegetables (optional)
1 cup chopped spinach (optional)
¼-½ cup soy powder
½ tsp dill weed
¼ tsp paprika

1. Sauté onion and celery in a small amount of water until soft. Add 2 cups water and/or stock, potatoes, carrots, and sea vegetables. Cover, bring to a boil, then simmer until vegetables are tender, about 15 minutes.
2. Add the spinach and cook just until limp. Sprinkle on the soy powder, dill weed, and paprika; stir in 3 cups water and/or stock; and heat through.

Vichyssoise (Leek and Potato Soup)

3 cups chopped well-cleaned leeks
1 cup chopped or thinly sliced onion
1 cup chopped celery (optional)
3 cups cubed potatoes
6 cups total water and/or stock
½ cup soy powder or 4 oz tofu, or 1 cup plain soy yogurt
⅛ tsp nutmeg
⅛ tsp white pepper
plain soy yogurt (p. 10), chopped chives or parsley, and hot sauce (optional)

1. Sauté leeks, onions, (and celery) in a small amount of water. Add potatoes and 2 cups of the liquid. Cover and simmer 30 minutes.
2. Add soy powder or tofu, nutmeg, and pepper. Purée and return to pot. Stir in remaining liquid. Cover and heat just until boiling.
3. Remove from heat; chill. If you like, blend in soy yogurt and garnish with chives, parsley, and/or hot sauce.

NEW ENGLAND-STYLE POTATO-MUSHROOM CHOWDER

12 medium potatoes, peeled and quartered
4 medium carrots, peeled and left whole
½ cup chopped parsley
chopped "stone soup" vegetable parts, such as celery tops,
    broccoli and cauliflower stems, cabbage cores
8 cups total water and/or stock
½ cup soy powder, thinned in hot broth, or 4-6 oz tofu
½ cup chopped reconstituted dried shiitake or other dried mushrooms (p. 13)
1 cup chopped fresh mushrooms
1-2 cloves garlic, pressed or finely chopped
2-4 tblsp medium or dark miso, thinned in hot broth

1. Place potatoes, carrots, parsley, and vegetable parts in water or stock. Cover and bring to a boil. Reduce heat and cook about an hour. Dissolve miso in a small amount of hot broth and set aside.
2. While soup cools, uncovered, sauté mushrooms and garlic in a small amount of the broth.
3. When soup is cool enough, remove carrots, slice, and set aside.
4. Purée potatoes and vegetable parts, along with soy powder or tofu, with a small amount of the broth, gradually adding more liquid. Return to soup pot. Add mushrooms and garlic, carrots and miso.
4. Return soup to a simmer and cook on low heat 10 more minutes.

MANHATTAN-STYLE POTATO-MUSHROOM CHOWDER

1. Omit the soy powder or tofu.
2. Substitute 1-2 tblsp hot sauce or ½-1 cup salsa for the miso.

MUSHROOM AND BARLEY SOUP

8 cups total water (with 2 tblsp vegetable broth powder, optional) and/or stock
½ cup barley
2 cups diced vegetables: carrots, celery, parsnips,
    broccoli and cauliflower stems, cabbage, rutabaga
1 bay leaf
2 cups diced potatoes
2 or more tblsp snipped or crumbled sea vegetables (optional)
3 cups sliced mushrooms
1 cup chopped or thinly sliced onions
¼ tsp each thyme and celery seed

1. In a covered pot, bring 4 cups liquid to a boil with the barley, diced vegetables, and bay leaf.
2. Reduce heat, cover, and simmer one hour or longer, until barley is soft.
3. Add potatoes and sea vegetables and cook 10 minutes.
4. Meanwhile, sauté mushrooms and onions in a small amount of water or stock. Add to soup with remaining liquid and herbs. Heat thoroughly.

QUICK VEGETABLE SOUP

4-5 cups total water (with 1 tblsp vegetable broth powder, optional) and/or stock
2 cups finely chopped or grated vegetables, such as cabbage, carrots, celery,
    onions, mushrooms, peppers, zucchini, and "stone soup" vegetable parts,
    such as cabbage cores and broccoli and cauliflower stems
2 cups chopped greens, such as beet tops, bok choy, celery tops, chard,
    parsley, spinach, watercress
⅓ cup whole wheat pastina or couscous
3 cloves garlic, pressed or finely chopped
½ cup total chopped parsley and/or sprouts
freshly ground black pepper

1. Boil the water or stock. Meanwhile, prepare the vegetables. (The metal blade of a food processor is perfect for the job.) Add to the boiling water, cover, return to a boil, reduce heat, and simmer 5 minutes.
2. Stir in the pastina or couscous. Again, bring to a boil, then simmer 5 minutes.
3. Add garlic, parsley, and sprouts. Return to a boil, add pepper, and serve—with hot sauce or tamari.

For a creamy soup, use a few tablespoons of soy powder. Make a paste first with a small amount of the hot soup.

Sweet and Sour Cabbage Soup

6 cups water (with 2 tblsp vegetable broth powder, optional) and/or stock
4 cups finely shredded green cabbage
1 cup chopped onion
2 cups shredded peeled apple
½ cup tomato juice, tomato sauce, crushed tomatoes, or tomato purée
2-4 tblsp lemon juice
2 tblsp rice syrup
¼ cup tamari
freshly ground black pepper

1. Heat water or stock to boiling in a large covered pot.
2. Add cabbage, onion, apple, and tomato.
3. Reduce heat and simmer 30 minutes.
4. Add lemon juice, rice syrup, tamari, and pepper, and serve.

Hot Potato-Hot Tomato-Cabbage Soup

2-3 cloves garlic, pressed or finely chopped
2 cups diced or chopped carrots
1 cup diced or chopped celery
1½ cups diced or chopped onion
3 cups shredded potatoes
4 cups shredded cabbage

6 cups total water and/or stock
¼ cup lemon juice
1 tblsp rice syrup
1 tblsp tamari
1 bay leaf
freshly ground black pepper

hot tomatoes: 4 cups total salsa and/or tomato sauce; or 6 fresh or a 28-oz can tomatoes, chopped, with a finely chopped chili or jalapeño pepper, hot sauce, hot pepper flakes, cayenne, and/or chili powder

1. The vegetables can be chopped and shredded with a food processor.
2. Combine everything in a large pot.
3. Cover, bring to a boil, reduce heat, and simmer 45 minutes to an hour, until the carrots and potatoes are tender.
4. Add more liquid if needed.

WINTER SQUASH AND POTATO SOUP

2 winter squash, such as acorn, buttercup, or butternut
2 cups finely chopped onion
1 cup finely chopped carrot
freshly ground black pepper
1 tblsp tamari
2 cups peeled, cubed potatoes
½ tsp each dried parsley and savory
½ tsp dill seed
¼ tsp celery seed
4 cups total water (with 2 tblsp vegetable broth powder, optional) and/or stock
mirin and nutmeg (optional)

1. Halve squash, remove seeds (to bake the seeds, see p. 212), and cut into ½-inch slices. Place in a steamer and cook for a few minutes, until the slices are just soft enough to peel easily. Peel and cube.
2. Heat a small amount of water or stock, and add carrots, onions, pepper, and tamari. Cover and simmer about 10 minutes, until vegetables are tender.
3. Add squash and potato cubes and 2 cups liquid. Simmer 25 minutes. (For a smooth soup, at this point purée in a blender or food processor, then return to pan.)
4. Add herbs, seeds, and remaining water, and heat through.
5. Serve with a few dashes of mirin and a sprinkle of nutmeg.

PUMPKIN OR WINTER SQUASH SOUP WITH MISO

2 onions, thinly sliced
3 cups peeled pumpkin or winter squash
   (buttercup, butternut, delicata), cut into ½-inch cubes
2 cups total water and/or stock
¼ tsp nutmeg
1 or more cloves garlic, pressed or finely chopped
4 tblsp dark miso
8 oz tofu, cut into ½-inch cubes (optional)
3 tblsp finely chopped fresh, or 1½ tblsp dried, parsley

1. Sauté onion in a small amount of water until wilted. Add pumpkin or squash and water and/or stock, cover, and bring to a boil. Reduce heat to low and simmer 25 minutes.
2. Stir in nutmeg, garlic, tofu, and miso thinned in a little of the hot soup. Return just to the boil; remove from heat.
3. For best flavor, cool to room temperature, then reheat, or refrigerate and reheat the next day, topped with parsley.

WINTER SQUASH AND APPLE SOUP

¼ cup finely sliced or finely chopped onion
1 clove garlic, pressed or finely chopped
3 cups peeled and cubed winter squash (buttercup, butternut, delicata)
2 cups total water and/or stock
1 cup apple juice or cider
½ cup diced apple
¼ tsp grated or ground nutmeg
freshly ground black pepper

1. Sauté onion and garlic in a small amount of water until soft, about 2 minutes. Add the squash and water or stock and bring to a boil.
2. Reduce heat, cover, and simmer until squash is soft, about 20 minutes.
3. Pour into blender or food processor and purée.
4. Return to pot, add juice or cider and blend until well combined. Stir in diced apple, nutmeg, and pepper and cook over low heat until heated through.

WARM GOLD SOUP

2 cups chopped onions
2 cloves garlic, pressed or finely chopped
½ cup or more chopped celery (and/or cabbage and broccoli
  or cauliflower stems)
3 cups peeled, chunked sweet potatoes or winter squash
  (buttercup, butternut, delicata)
3-4 cups total water (with 1 tblsp vegetable broth powder, optional) and/or stock
1 bay leaf
1 tsp each paprika, turmeric, and basil
dash each cinnamon, cayenne, and freshly ground black pepper
1 cup chopped fresh or canned tomatoes
½ cup chopped bell pepper
1½ cups cooked chickpeas
1 tblsp tamari

1. Heat a small amount of water or stock in a large pot. Sauté onions, garlic, and celery until soft. Add sweet potatoes or squash and cook another 5 minutes, stirring occasionally.
2. Add 3 cups water/stock and spices. Cover, bring to a boil, reduce heat, and simmer 15 minutes.
3. Stir in tomatoes, bell pepper, chickpeas, and tamari, and cook another 10 minutes. Add remaining water if needed.

Black Bean Soup

1 cup black beans, soaked (see below)
7 cups total water (with 2 tblsp vegetable broth powder, optional) and/or stock
1 large onion, finely chopped
2 cloves garlic, pressed or finely chopped
½ cup finely diced carrots
¼ cup diced celery (and/or cabbage and broccoli and cauliflower stems)
2-4 tblsp snipped or crumbled sea vegetables (optional)
¾ tsp crushed cumin seed
freshly ground black pepper
chopped scallions or chives

1. Cover beans with water and soak at least 8 hours, or boil for 2 minutes and let stand 1 hour.
2. Drain beans, add water or stock, bring to boil, reduce heat and simmer, partly covered, for 2-3 hours, until beans are soft.
3. In a separate pan, sauté the onions and garlic in a small amount of water until transparent. Add carrots, celery, and sea vegetables, and cook, stirring, a few more minutes. Add the vegetables to the beans. Stir in cumin and pepper and simmer 30 more minutes.
4. If you want a smooth soup, purée in batches in a food mill or processor.
5. Serve garnished with chopped scallions or chives.

Chickpea and Pasta Soup

¾ cup finely chopped onion
1 tsp fresh chopped, ½ tsp dried, thyme
2 cups chopped fresh tomatoes or a 16-oz can tomatoes, chopped
2 cloves garlic, pressed or finely chopped
2-4 cups total water (with 1½ tsp vegetable broth powder, optional) and/or stock
2 cups cooked chickpeas
½ cup cooked small pasta (orzo, shells, elbows, etc.)
½ tsp each turmeric and crushed cumin seeds
freshly ground black pepper

1. In a large pan, sauté the onion and thyme in a small amount of water until onion is soft.
2. Add the tomatoes, their juice, and the garlic, and simmer 15 minutes, stirring occasionally.
3. Add water or stock and chickpeas, and simmer another 15 minutes, stirring occasionally.
4. Add pasta, herbs, and pepper, and heat through.

AASH: IRANIAN FOUR-BEAN AND VEGETABLE SOUP

¼ cup each kidney, lima, and pinto beans
1 large onion or equivalent, chopped
4 cloves garlic, chopped
1 tblsp curry powder
6+ cups total water and/or stock
½ cup lentils
1 tblsp whole wheat flour
2 cups pasta
1 cup sliced beets
2 cups chopped spinach, beet tops, chard, or kale
2-4 tblsp vinegar or lemon juice
¼ cup soy powder (optional)
1 cup chopped dried apricots (optional)

1. To reduce cooking time for the kidney, lima, and pinto beans, soak them in water all day or overnight.
2. In a large pot, sauté the onion in a small amount of water or stock until soft. Add garlic and sauté until both are golden. Stir in the curry.
3. Add beans to the pot with 6 cups of water and/or stock.
4. Cover, bring to a boil, and cook 30- 45 minutes for soaked beans or 1-1½ hours for unsoaked.
5. Add lentils and continue cooking until all four beans are almost fully cooked, about 45 more minutes.
6. Add more water at any time if needed.
7. Dissolve the flour in cold water and stir in. Boil a few minutes, then add pasta and beets. Cook about 15 more minutes, until pasta and beets are tender.
8. Add greens, vinegar or lemon juice (and soy powder and apricots), and cook five more minutes.

Pasta and Bean Soup

1 cup chopped onions
2-4 cloves garlic, pressed or finely chopped
4 tblsp chopped fresh, or 2 tblsp dry, parsley
2 tblsp chopped fresh, or 1 tblsp dry, basil;
   or 1 tsp each dried basil, oregano, thyme
2½-3 cups chopped fresh or canned tomatoes
several dashes hot sauce
7½ cups total water (with 2 tblsp vegetable broth powder, optional) and/or stock
1½ cups cooked or canned white beans, such as great northern or navy
2 cups uncooked pasta
freshly ground black pepper

1. Sauté onions and garlic in a small amount of water until transparent.
2. Add parsley and herbs; simmer one minute. Add tomatoes and hot sauce; simmer 5 minutes.
3. Add water or stock and beans; simmer 15 minutes. Bring to a boil.
4. Add pasta and cook 8 minutes or until desired tenderness. Season with pepper.

Minestrone

Add:

1 cup diced or sliced celery
2 cups diced or sliced carrots
2 cups finely diced potatoes

along with water or stock.

Cook until the vegetables are tender.
You can also add these or other vegetables or combinations:

1 cup each sliced mushrooms and leeks
1 cup fresh corn kernels and ½ cup chopped okra
1 cup each sliced or diced zucchini and shredded cabbage
1 cup small broccoli florets and chopped stems and ½ cup diced peeled turnip

LENTIL SOUP

2 cups chopped or thinly sliced onion
2-3 cloves garlic, pressed or finely chopped
3 carrots, coarsely grated
1 cup chopped celery (and/or cabbage and broccoli or cauliflower stems)
¾ tsp each marjoram, thyme, and basil
2 whole cloves (optional)
4 cups chopped fresh tomatoes or a 28-oz can tomatoes, chopped
7 cups water (with 2 tblsp vegetable broth powder, optional) or stock
1 tblsp snipped or crumbled sea vegetables (optional)
2 bay leaves
1½ cups dried lentils
freshly ground black pepper
1/4 cup chopped fresh, or 2 tblsp dried, parsley

1. Sauté onion, garlic, carrots, celery, marjoram, thyme, basil, and cloves in a small amount of water for 5 minutes. Add tomatoes, their juice, water or stock, sea vegetables, bay leaves, and lentils. Bring to a boil, reduce heat, cover, and simmer about 1 hour or until lentils are soft.
2. Add pepper and parsley and simmer a few more minutes.

Note: Other beans or bean combinations can be substituted for the lentils.

QUICK AND SPICY LENTIL SOUP

1 cup chopped or thinly sliced onion
2 cloves garlic, pressed or finely chopped
½ tsp cumin seed, ground in a spice mill or mortar and pestle
¼ tsp each ground cloves, ginger, and nutmeg
⅛ tsp each cinnamon and cayenne
freshly ground black pepper
7 cups water
1 cup lentils

1. Sauté onion, garlic, and spices in just enough water until onion is soft.
2. Add remaining water and lentils. Cover, bring to a boil, then simmer 1½ hours.
3. *If you like your soup smooth,* separate the lentils from most of the liquid, use a blender or processor to purée them, then reunite puréed lentils and remaining liquid.

HEARTiest Pea Soup

2 cups dried split peas
6 cups water
½ cup barley (optional)
½ cup dried white beans, such as fava, navy, or lima (optional)
4 cups water (with 1 tblsp vegetable broth powder, optional) and/or stock
1 cup thinly sliced onions
2 cloves garlic, pressed or finely chopped
1 stalk celery, sliced (optional)
¼ cup thinly sliced leeks (optional)
2 broccoli stems, thinly sliced (optional)
1 cup total chunked potato and/or turnip or rutabaga
1 cup thickly sliced carrots
2-4 tblsp total sea vegetables: hijiki, wakame, arame
   (snipped with a scissors or crumbled)
½ tsp each dill weed, dill seed, tarragon, thyme
¼ tsp celery seed
2 bay leaves
freshly ground black pepper
2 tblsp dark miso
hot sauce

1. Bring peas and 6 cups water to a boil in a large pot. Boil several minutes, stir in beans and barley, then let sit while you prepare the vegetables.
2. Add 4 cups water or stock, onions, garlic, celery, leeks, and broccoli stems. Bring to a boil, then reduce heat and simmer 1 hour.
3. Grind dill, tarragon, and thyme in a spice mill or mortar and pestle.
4. Add with remaining ingredients except miso and hot sauce. Cook another 30 minutes, until the peas are dissolved and the beans and barley are soft.
5. Remove from heat and stir in miso. Serve with hot sauce.
6. Like all soups, this tastes even better when reheated the next day. It will thicken; add water.

This soup, with Johnnycakes (p. 38), hits the spot when you return, weary but mellow, from an aerobic afternoon of cross-country skiing or snowshoeing.

VEGETABLE SANDWICHES

Slice (and toast) wholegrain bread, or heat whole wheat pita just until soft and warm and cut in half to make pockets. Spread one side with miso and the other with mustard or tahini. Stuff with greens; alfalfa, red clover, or other sprouts; sliced or chopped onions or scallions, mushrooms, bell peppers, and/or tomatoes; grated carrots; and/or any other vegetables you have on hand and think would taste good. Or just use leftover salad. Squeeze on lemon or lime juice, and/or sprinkle on hot sauce and/or freshly ground black pepper.

Along with the vegetables, you can also add plain or marinated broiled tempeh (p. 138), cooked chickpeas (p. 5), hummus (p. 73), tofu spread (p. 71), tabouli (p. 74), dips (p. 71-73), dolmadakias (p. 98), eggplant relish (p. 148), any kind of vegetable/ grain/tofu burger (p. 120, 129, 136, and 226), slices of lentil loaf (p. 120), etc.

Another approach is to finely chop all the vegetables and combine them in a bowl. Toss them with salsa or salsa-tomato sauce mix, or with miso and mustard, and then put on the bread or in the pita. This was our dinner almost every night during seven months of travel in New Zealand and four months in national parks and monuments of the American southwest.

FRUIT SANDWICHES

1. Slice apples, pears, nectarines, plums, peaches, apricots, bananas, melon, mangos, papayas, or whatever is most readily available or in season wherever you happen to be.
2. Section oranges and/or other sectionable fruit.
3. Halve or slice large grapes or berries; leave smaller ones whole.
4. Spread rice syrup on one slice of wholegrain bread or one side of a pita pocket and tahini on the other. Fill with fruit. Or, make open-face sandwiches using rice cakes or fat- and sweet-free wholegrain crackers, such as Wasa or RyVita.
5. This was our tailgate, picnic, trailside, or bicycle roadside lunch almost every day on those same trips.

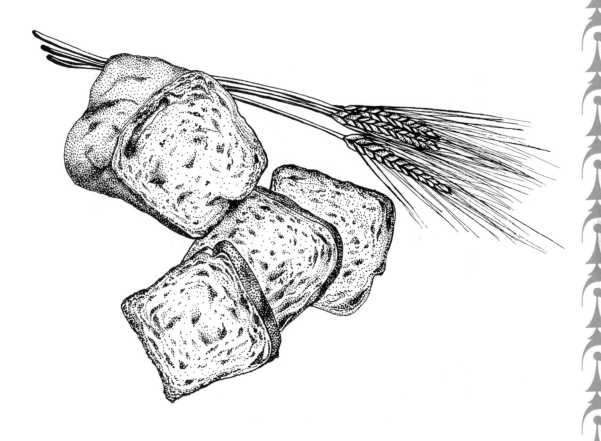

TOFU OR BEAN SANDWICH SPREAD OR DIP

Mash or purée in a food processor:

8 oz tofu, 2 tblsp lemon or lime juice or brown rice vinegar, and any one or combination of vegetables, condiments, and herbs from these lists:
⅓ cup finely chopped bell pepper, celery, onion, parsley, other vegetables
1 or 2 cloves garlic, pressed or finely chopped
2-4 tblsp miso (more if light and sweet; less if medium, or dark and thick)
1-2 tblsp each tahini and tamari
1 tsp (more or less) dried parsley, basil, summer savory, marjoram, dill, turmeric, curry, celery seed, mustard (or prepared mustard), cayenne, other herbs and spices
1 tblsp prepared horseradish
freshly ground black pepper
dash mirin

For example:
One Saturday afternoon in winter, you might purée together for lunchtime pita sandwiches:

8 oz tofu	1 clove garlic, pressed
2 tblsp lemon or lime juice	2 tblsp barley miso
⅓ cup finely chopped onion	1 tsp dried dill
⅓ cup finely chopped parsley	freshly ground black pepper

1. You could spread mustard on the pita, stuff the sandwiches with sprouts, greens, and sliced mushrooms, as described on p. 70, prepare a couple of glasses of carrot juice or use some thawed all morning from the freezer, and sit down to a delicious lunch.
2. Or, the tofu purée can be served in a bowl as dip for a platter of raw vegetables: carrot, celery, cucumber, and zucchini sticks; broccoli and cauliflower florets; sliced mushrooms, bell peppers, and radishes; green onions; green or wax beans, etc.

Bean spread or dip

1½ cups of any cooked beans, such as black, kidney, navy, pinto, red, or soy, (or one can, drained) can be used in place of the tofu.

Red Lentil Dip

2 cups cooked red or orange lentils (p. 5)
4 or more cloves garlic, pressed or finely chopped
½ cup chopped onion
2 tblsp lemon or lime juice
1½ tsp ground cumin
freshly ground black pepper
2 tablespoons finely chopped fresh, or 1 tblsp dried, parsley

1. Mash lentils and mix with remaining ingredients.
2. Or, to make best use of a food processor, toss in the peeled garlic with the metal blade spinning.
3. When garlic is minced, add one small onion or half a larger one and the fresh parsley. Chop briefly.
4. Then add remaining ingredients and purée.
Instead of blending in the fresh parsley, it can be used as a garnish if you're using the dip on crackers or bread.

Bean/Salsa Sandwich Spread or Dip

cooked beans - aduki, kidney, black, or other cut-up fresh vegetables
salsa or salsa/tomato sauce mix
corn tortillas or no-oil tortilla chips

1. Mash together beans and salsa, or purée in a processor. Place in a bowl.
2. Arrange vegetables on a platter. If using tortillas, toast them and break into pieces. Go for it!

Denya's Hummus

1½-2 cups cooked chickpeas (p. 5)   2-4 tblsp lemon juice
1 clove garlic, pressed or finely chopped   ¼-½ cup water
3-4 tblsp tahini

1. Purée in blender or processor until absolutely smooth. (Add just enough water for desired consistency.) If using a processor, first drop in the garlic with the metal blade spinning, then add remaining ingredients.
2. Any or all of these can be added to the basic recipe (let the processor chop the vegetables first): ¼ cup finely chopped onion, ¼ cup chopped parsley, freshly ground black pepper, ¼-½ tsp dill, ¼ tsp ground cumin, 1 tblsp tamari.
3. Use as a sandwich spread or dip for vegetables.

Tabouli - Middle Eastern Bulgur Salad

3 cups cooked bulgur wheat (p. 3), or quinoa (p. 4)—
  for an Andean bulgur salad
1 cup finely chopped onion and/or scallions
1-2 garlic cloves, pressed or finely chopped
½ cup finely chopped fresh mint leaves
  or 1-2 tblsp peppermint or spearmint tea leaves
1 cup finely chopped fresh, or ⅓ cup dried, parsley
1 tblsp minced fresh, or 1½ tsp dried, basil, marjoram, or oregano
2 cups chopped tomatoes
4-6 tblsp lemon juice
freshly ground black pepper

1. Toss all ingredients in a bowl.
2. Eat now or chill.
Tabouli makes great pita sandwiches (see p. 70).

Baba Ganouj - Lebanese Eggplant Dip or Spread

4-5 cups chunked peeled eggplant (1 large)
3 tblsp tahini
2 cloves garlic, minced or finely chopped
2 tblsp chopped fresh, or 2 tsp dried, parsley
¼ cup chopped onion
tamari and/or freshly ground black pepper to taste
¼ cup lemon juice
ground cumin and/or cayenne to taste (optional)

1. Steam eggplant 15-20 minutes, until soft.
2. Mash all ingredients together.
3. *Or*, mince garlic in a food processor by dropping it in with the metal blade
   spinning. Add onion and chop, then add remaining ingredients and purée.

Eggplant/Tomato Salad

4-5 cups chunked peeled eggplant (1 large)
1 cup chopped onion
1½ cups chopped celery
1 cup chopped bell pepper
½ cup chopped tomato
½ cup chopped mushrooms
1½ cups total salsa and/or tomato sauce
1/4 cup red wine vinegar
freshly ground black pepper
¼ cup red wine vinegar

1. Steam eggplant 15-20 minutes, until soft.
2. Mix with remaining ingredients, cover, and marinate in refrigerator until cold.

Couscous Salad

3 cups cooked couscous (p. 3)
2 tblsp chopped fresh, or 1 tblsp dried, dill
2-4 tblsp lemon or lime juice
cayenne to taste
2 or more garlic cloves, pressed or finely chopped
freshly ground black pepper to taste
½ cup chopped fresh, or 2 tblsp dried, parsley

Combine everything in a bowl; mix lightly.

It's good warm or cold.

Optional Replacements or Additions:

chopped green onions or chives, diced tomatoes, diced cucumbers, cooked chickpeas, prepared mustard, ground coriander seeds

Pasta Salad

cooked pasta (p. 89)
chopped bell peppers, celery, cucumbers, mushrooms, onions or scallions,
   parsley, tomatoes, etc.
grated carrots
pressed or finely chopped garlic
miso or tamari
mustard or tahini
balsamic vinegar, brown rice vinegar, or wine vinegar
herbs: celery seed, dill weed and/or seed, savory
freshly ground black pepper

Toss everything together.

Or, combine the pasta and vegetables in a bowl and toss with salsa.

Curried Tempeh Salad

Toss:

1 package (8 oz) tempeh, cubed
¼ cup chopped onion or scallion
1 cup shredded red or green cabbage
¼-½ cup each of any or all: chopped cucumber, bell pepper, celery, parsley, mushrooms,
   zucchini; grated carrot; small florets of broccoli and cauliflower; peas; other vegetables
½ cup chopped apple
¼ cup raisins or currants

Blend, then either pour over salad and toss, or serve separately:

1 cup soy yogurt (p. 10)
2 tsp curry powder
3 tblsp lemon or lime juice

1 tblsp prepared mustard
¼ tsp celery seed
freshly ground black pepper

Potato Salad

¼-½ cup finely chopped sweet onions, red onions, or scallions
¼ cup diced cucumber
½ cup finely chopped celery
½ cup shredded, grated, or finely chopped carrots
½ cup diced bell peppers
2 or more cloves garlic, pressed or finely chopped
¼ cup chopped fresh, or 2 tblsp dried, parsley
½ cup chopped pickles and 2-4 tblsp pickle juice (optional)
2-4 tblsp prepared mustard
1 tsp fresh dill, or ½ tsp dried dill or dill seeds
½ tsp paprika
½ tsp celery seed
thyme or summer savory, fresh or dried (optional)
freshly ground black pepper

optional:
2 cups plain soy yogurt (p. 10), tofu "mayonnaise (p. 147), or
   1 tblsp miso blended with 3 tblsp vinegar: balsamic, brown rice, or wine
4 cups warm cubed steamed potatoes

1. Combine all but the potatoes in a large bowl.
   (Other chopped vegetables, such as beans, broccoli, cabbage,
   cauliflower, greens, mushrooms, peas, sea vegetables, and
   sprouts can replace or augment the listed vegetables.)
2. Fold in the warm potatoes and chill thoroughly before serving.

VEGETABLE-BEAN SALAD WITH RICE OR PASTA

Salad

3 cups cooked brown rice (p. 2) or orzo (p. 89)
2 cups chopped edible pod peas and/or celery
2 cups cooked kidney beans or chickpeas (p. 5)
2 cups thinly sliced mushrooms
florets and sliced stems of 1 head broccoli, steamed until bright green
1 bell pepper, diced
4-6 thinly sliced scallions

Dressing

2 tblsp lemon juice	1 tsp dry mustard
3 tblsp vinegar - balsamic, rice, or wine	¾ tsp tarragon
2-3 cloves garlic, pressed or minced	freshly ground black pepper

1. Combine all the salad ingredients in a large bowl.
2. Combine all the dressing ingredients in a jar. Cover and shake well. Pour over salad and toss to mix thoroughly. Refrigerate.

CHICKPEA SALAD WITH RAW VEGETABLES

2 cups cooked (or canned) chickpeas (p. 5)
½ cup finely chopped onion, scallions, or green onions
½ cup sliced celery
½ cup chopped parsley
1-2 cloves garlic, pressed or finely chopped
other chopped fresh vegetables, such as bell pepper, carrot, cucumber, mushrooms
freshly ground black pepper
1-2 tblsp prepared mustard (optional)
½ tsp tarragon or basil
2-4 tblsp total vinegar (balsamic, brown rice, cider, or wine) and/or lemon or lime juice

Combine all ingredients; chill.

CHICKPEA SALAD WITH COOKED VEGETABLES

1 cup chopped onion
2 cloves garlic,
   pressed or finely chopped
3 cups zucchini,
   cut in quarter-rounds
2 cups broccoli florets
   and sliced tender stems
2 tsp dried basil
1 tsp dried tarragon
freshly ground black pepper

2 cups cooked or canned chickpeas
3 tblsp lemon or lime juice
1 tblsp tamari (optional)
½ cup diced tomato
¼ cup diced bell pepper
¼ cup chopped fresh parsley

1. Sauté vegetables briefly in a small amount of water. Stir in basil, tarragon, and pepper.
2. Mix with chickpeas, lemon juice, and tamari in a bowl. Toss or garnish with tomato, bell pepper and parsley.

MINTED CAULIFLOWER SALAD

1 head cauliflower, broken into florets and steamed until crisp-tender
½ cup chopped fresh mint leaves,
   or 1-2 tblsp dried peppermint or spearmint leaves
1 clove garlic, pressed or finely chopped
⅓ cup wine vinegar
freshly ground black pepper

1. Place steamed cauliflower in a bowl. Mix with the mint and garlic.
2. Chill. Toss with the vinegar and pepper.

GRAIN AND VEGETABLE SALAD

Salad

3 cups cooked grain, such as barley, quinoa, or brown rice (p. 2)
1 cup each thinly sliced carrot and diced bell pepper
½ cup diced red, Vidalia, or other sweet onions, or scallions
¼ cup chopped fresh, or 1 tblsp dried, dill
¼ cup chopped fresh, or 1 tblsp dried, parsley

Dressing

2 cloves garlic, pressed or finely chopped
¼ cup total balsamic, red wine, or other vinegar, and/or lemon or lime juice
¼ tsp dill seed
⅛ tsp celery seed
freshly ground black pepper

1. While the grain cooks, prepare the vegetables and combine the dressing ingredients in a large bowl.
2. When the grain is done, add it to the dressing and mix well.
3. Add the remaining salad ingredients and toss.

LENTIL SALAD

2 cups raw lentils
6 cups water
2 cloves garlic, pressed or finely chopped
1 cup finely chopped onion
½ tsp each cloves, cumin, curry, tarragon, thyme—
   ground in a spice mill or mortar and pestle
1 bay leaf

1. Combine in a pot, bring to a boil, then simmer, covered, about 20 minutes, until lentils are tender but not mushy.
2. Cool slightly. Add and mix well:

¼ cup finely chopped fresh, or 2 tblsp dried, parsley
½ cup each chopped carrots and tomatoes (optional)
2 tblsp wine vinegar
freshly ground black pepper

Serve warm or cold, with hot sauce.

THREE-BEAN SALAD

1½ cups each green beans and wax beans, cut into 1-inch pieces
1½ cups cooked kidney beans (p. 11), or one 15-oz can, drained
½ cup each diced bell pepper, celery, and onion

Dressing

⅔ cup vinegar: balsamic, brown rice, cider, or wine
1 or 2 cloves garlic, pressed or finely chopped
2 tblsp rice syrup
1 tblsp chopped fresh, or 1 tsp dried, garden herbs, such as basil, dill,
   marjoram, oregano, parsley, savory, tarragon, or thyme
freshly ground black pepper

1. Steam fresh beans until crisp-tender, about 5 minutes.
   Combine with kidney beans and vegetables.
2. Combine the dressing ingredients, add to bean mixture, and toss well.
3. Chill at least an hour.

WALDORF SALAD

chopped apples
grated or shredded carrots
shredded or finely chopped celery
crushed pineapple or tidbits, drained,
  or minced fresh pineapple
raisins or currants
alfalfa, red clover, or other sprouts
chopped fresh or dried apricots
  (optional)
grated cabbage (optional)
lemon juice (optional)
rice syrup
soy yogurt (p. 10)

1. Toss everything together.
2. *Or* toss everything except the soy yogurt, serve the salad in small bowls,
   and spoon the yogurt over.
3. *Or* combine rice syrup and soy yogurt to make a dressing to spoon over
   the served salad.

DILLED CUCUMBERS WITH SOY YOGURT

cucumbers—peeled, cut lengthwise into halves or quarters, and thinly sliced
Combine in a bowl, mix well, and toss with cucumbers:
soy yogurt (p. 10)
garlic, minced or finely chopped
finely chopped fresh dill
cayenne and ground cumin
wine vinegar or cider vinegar
chopped fresh mint leaves and hot sauce (optional)

TOFU "FETA" (AND SPINACH SALAD)

8 oz tofu, pressed (p. 6) and diced

Sauce:

¼ cup chick pea miso, any light miso, or any miso
1 tblsp lemon juice
1 tblsp white wine vinegar or brown rice vinegar
1 tblsp mirin (optional)
2 tsp prepared mustard
2 cloves garlic, pressed or finely chopped
½ tsp dried herbs, such as basil, rosemary, savory, tarragon,
    and/or thyme (optional)
2-4 tblsp water

1. Blend miso with lemon juice, vinegar, and mirin. Stir in mustard, garlic, and
   herbs. Add water to desired thinness. Fold in diced tofu.
   Chill until ready to serve.
2. Prepare a big, green salad (p. 144) Serve with tofu "feta," vinegar or salad
   dressing (p. 145-147), and croutons (below). Spinach salad with feta is a
   Greek specialty. *Or*, eat salad with feta as a pita sandwich.

CROUTONS

Toast slices of whole grain bread. Cube with a knife.

CRUMBLY SCRAMBLED TOFU OR OKARA

¾ cup diced onion
3-4 cups diced vegetables, such as bell pepper, broccoli, carrots, celery, corn, garlic,
    green beans, kale, kohlrabi, mushrooms, parsley, peas, radishes,
    sea vegetables, summer squash
½ lb (8 oz) tofu, crumbled (7)*
2 tsp tamari
½ tsp each turmeric and dill weed
freshly ground black pepper

1. Heat a small amount of water in a skillet. Add onion and other vegetables and
   sauté 3-4 minutes until onion is soft. Add tofu, tamari, turmeric, and pepper.
2. Sauté over medium heat for about 5 minutes, stirring constantly, until tofu is
   light, dry, and almost fluffy.

Okara (p. 16) can be substituted for some or all of the tofu.

WORLD'S FASTEST SNACK, LUNCH, OR DINNER

raw vegetables (see below)
faultless, shortening-free pretzels
mustard

1. Prepare raw vegetables: carrot, celery, cucumber, and zucchini sticks; broccoli
   and cauliflower florets; bell pepper, mushroom, and radish slices; green onions,
   green or wax beans, tomatoes, etc.
2. Place pretzels in a bowl.
3. Open the mustard, dip in the vegetables and pretzels, and challenge yourself to
   stop before you are overstuffed.

TAKE-ALONG LUNCH

It's simple to bring along your own healthful foods, and you can feel good about packing your snacks and lunch in containers that you rinse and reuse.

Get a nylon lunchbag with velcro closure. It will last for literally decades. The heart of your lunch can be leftovers—grain, vegetable, salad—packed in one or more reusable plastic containers. There's no need to buy new ones; save tubs and lids from miso or other food you can't get in bulk. Bring along a fork; a sturdy plastic one will also last for years and you won't feel bad if you lose it.

Bring some kind of faultless no-fat wholegrain bread, cracker, muffin, pretzel, etc. in a reusable bag. Real bagels contain no shortening. Even week-old whole wheat or multigrain bagels taste bakery-fresh when baked or toasted in the morning and taken along with your lunch.

Take a whole organic carrot, or a peeled one cut into sticks, and other fresh vegetables: celery, cucumber, tomatoes, etc.

For your beverage, instead of repeatedly buying those tiny boxes or cans, buy a reusable container once, and you can use it forever. Each day, refill it with fruit juice or vanilla or carob soymilk. In cold weather, take a thermos of herbal tea or grain beverage.

Take some washed whole fruits: apple, pear, stone fruit, citrus fruit, organic grapes. To save time during your lunch or snack break, you can peel and section grapefruits, oranges, mandarins, clementines, etc. in advance and put them in a reusable container, or cut the oranges into quarters or sixths.

If you have some leftover dessert, pack that, too.

If you have to get out early in the morning, you can prepare lunches the night before.

GRAINS, VEGETABLES, AND LEGUMES

PASTA

BROWN RICE AND...

OTHER GRAINS

BEANS

TOFU

Any grain, vegetable, or legume dish served with a large, fresh green salad, makes a delicious, nutritious, and filling dinner.

PASTA

Bring about 5 quarts water to a full, rolling boil. Stir in 1-2 pounds (2-8 cups) whole-grain or vegetable pasta: orzo, shells, elbows, spirals, flats, spaghetti, or any of the other shapes and sizes you find at a food coop or the bulk section of a natural foods store. Udon (brown rice and wheat flour noodles) and soba (buckwheat noodles) can be used just like pasta. The smaller, denser pasta, when cooked, will fill up more space for the uncooked volume; for example, 1 cup raw orzo yields 3 cups cooked, 1 cup elbows yields about 2 cups cooked, and 1 cup spirals yields 1½ cups cooked.

Return to a lively boil, reduce heat just enough so the pot doesn't boil over, and keep boiling 8-15 minutes, depending on the thickness of the pasta, until just tender. Pour into a colander and drain. Return to the pot and cover to keep it hot.

Use a large spoon or ladle, or a small bowl, to scoop the pasta out of the pot and onto the plate.

Top with heated unsweetened, oil-free, thickener-free salsa or a mix of salsa and tomato sauce. As you're heating the salsa/tomato sauce, you can add more garlic or onions, and/or sliced or chopped mushrooms, bell peppers, celery, summer squash, broccoli, carrots, kale, Swiss chard, fresh tomatoes, or other vegetables. Or, briefly steam or sauté these vegetables first and then add the salsa and heat. You can also add cubed tofu or tempeh to the salsa.

You can also toss the hot pasta with miso and tahini, or with a sauce made by blending and heating miso, tahini, brown rice vinegar, and garlic, and thinning with water.

Try alternating plates of tomato-, salsa-, or squash-sauce-topped and miso-tahini-topped pasta. With a large, fresh salad, this is a dinner you wish you could have every night, if there weren't so many other wonderful things to have. If you make enough, the leftovers are also a great lunch the next day, even brought to work, school, or picnic cold in a container.

TOMATO SAUCE

1 cup chopped onion
1 cup chopped celery, stalks and leaves
½ cup chopped carrot
½ cup chopped bell pepper
2 cloves garlic, chopped or pressed
6 cups coarsely chopped fresh or canned tomatoes (one 28-oz can)
1 sprig fresh or ½ tsp dried herbs, any or all: basil, marjoram, oregano, parsley, savory, tarragon, thyme
1 tsp rice syrup
freshly ground black pepper

1. Sauté onion, celery, carrot, pepper, and garlic about 5 minutes.
2. Add tomatoes, herbs, rice syrup, and pepper.
3. Cook gently, uncovered, about 45 minutes, stirring occasionally. If using canned tomatoes, cook only about 15 minutes.

TOMATO SAUCE PLUS

Add broccoli florets, sliced mushrooms, sliced summer squash, and/or other raw vegetables during the last few minutes of cooking, or if you prepared the sauce in advance, add the vegetables when reheating it.

UNCOOKED TOMATO SAUCE

3 cloves garlic, pressed or finely chopped
2 cups chopped tomatoes
3 tblsp chopped fresh, or 1½ tblsp dried, basil*
dash cayenne or 2 tblsp red wine vinegar

1. Combine garlic and tomatoes in a blender. Stir in basil and cayenne.
2. If using a food processor, drop in garlic cloves with metal blade spinning.
3. When minced, add tomatoes. Transfer to another container and add basil and cayenne or vinegar.

*Other herbs, such as marjoram, oregano, parsley, rosemary, savory, and thyme can be used in place of, or in addition to, the basil.

See also: Gazpacho (p. 53)

PESTO

Fat-free "pesto" can be made instantly in the food processor, and kept indefinitely
   in the freezer in small amounts, wrapped in squares of waxed paper.

1. Drop garlic cloves in with the metal blade spinning.
2. Add fresh basil leaves and purée. Proportions are 4-6 garlic cloves for
   24 large basil leaves.
3. Toss it into cooked pasta by itself or along with tomato sauce or a
   miso-tahini sauce.

WINTER SQUASH SAUCE

4 cups winter squash or pumpkin purée (p. 161)
stock from cooking the squash or pumpkin
1 cup sliced onions
1 cup sliced or chopped mushrooms
2-4 cloves garlic, pressed or finely chopped
1 tblsp parsley
¼ tsp each crushed sage, rosemary, and thyme
⅟₁₆ tsp white pepper, or freshly ground black pepper
¼-inch cubes of pressed tofu (optional)

1. Sauté onions, mushrooms, garlic, herbs, and pepper in a small amount of stock
   until vegetables are soft.
2. Thin the squash or pumpkin by blending it with up to 1 cup of stock.
3. Add the purée to the sautéed vegetables and herbs and heat through.
4. Fold in tofu cubes.
5. Serve over cooked pasta, with a salad.

SWEET WINTER SQUASH SAUCE

1. Heat cooked winter squash with crushed pineapple, chopped apples, and
   raisins. If liquid is needed, use orange juice.
2. Serve over cooked pasta. It's a main course noodle pudding.

PASTA AND WINTER SQUASH "HELPER"

thinly sliced onions
pressed or finely chopped garlic
thinly sliced mushrooms
snipped or crumbled sea vegetables (optional)
winter squash, partly steamed, peeled, and cubed
cooked pasta
miso, thinned in hot water or stock from steaming the squash
tahini
white pepper -or- mirin and/or brown rice vinegar

1. Sauté onions, garlic, mushrooms (and sea vegetables) in a small amount of water or stock.
2. Add cubed squash with a bit more water or stock, and cook and stir a few minutes.
3. Stir in pasta, thinned miso, tahini and pepper or vinegar.
4. Cook until pasta and squash are coated with sauce and everything is piping hot.

PASTA WITH WINTER SQUASH AND SPICY SAUCE

cooked spaghetti or other pasta
1 winter squash, such as buttercup, butternut, delicata, Hokkaido, baby Hubbard
spicy sauce (see p. 93)

1. Halve the squash and remove the seeds (to bake the seeds, see p. 212).
2. Then cut the squash into smaller pieces and steam until beginning to soften.
3. Let cool and use a knife or large spoon to remove squash from rind as you would separate melon from rind. (For some varieties, it's easier to peel the rind from the squash.)
4. Cut into chunks and return to steamer.
5. Meanwhile, prepare the spicy sauce (p. 93).
6. When sauce is ready, place pasta on plate, top with reheated squash chunks, and ladle sauce over all. Add a salad and you have dinner.

SPICY SAUCE

¼ cup cornstarch (or arrowroot or kuzu: see p. 13)
1½ cups lukewarm water
¼ cup tamari
2 cloves garlic, pressed or finely chopped
⅛ tsp cayenne pepper
½ tsp grated fresh, or ¼ tsp dried, ginger
1 cup thinly sliced mushrooms
½ cup thinly sliced onions

1. Combine all except the mushrooms and onions in a saucepan. Cook on medium high heat, stirring constantly, until sauce thickens and becomes translucent.
3. Now stir in the mushrooms and onions, and heat a few more minutes.

PASTA AND VEGETABLES WITH TAHINI SAUCE

1-2 cloves garlic,
  pressed or finely chopped
3 tblsp tahini
3 tblsp balsamic vinegar
1 tsp ground cumin
6 tblsp water

1 cup sliced carrots
½ cup sliced scallions or onions
4 cups broccoli florets and sliced stems
about 6 cups cooked orzo
  or other small pasta
freshly ground black pepper

1. Combine garlic, tahini, vinegar, cumin, and water.
2. Steam carrots, onions, and broccoli (or stir-fry in a small amount of water) just until crisp-tender. Stir in dressing, pasta, and pepper.

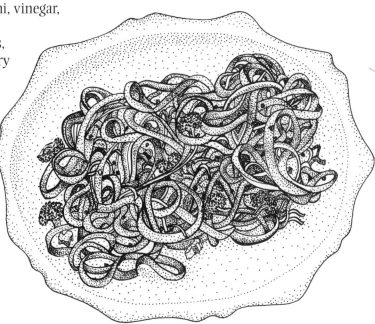

Stovetop Eggplant Parmigiana

1 eggplant, diced and steamed
  (peeling is optional)
4 cups cooked small pasta
3 cups chopped onions
2-4 cups total diced fresh or
  canned tomatoes, tomato sauce, and/or salsa

1 tblsp grated fresh ginger
1 tsp rice syrup
1 tblsp tamari
freshly ground black pepper

1. Sauté onions until soft and golden in a small amount of water in a large nonstick skillet. Add eggplant, tomatoes, and ginger, and cook a few minutes.
2. Add rice syrup, tamari, and pepper, and heat through.
3. Stir in pasta.

Pasta Primavera

cooked and drained pasta
quartered mushrooms
sliced zucchini and/or yellow crookneck squash
other possibilities: broccoli and cauliflower florets, 1-inch pieces of green and
  waxed beans, peas, chunked eggplant, chopped green onions

garlic, pressed or finely chopped
bell pepper, cut in strips
sliced onion

1. Steam vegetables or stir-fry in a small amount of water until crisp-tender:
2. Toss with cooked pasta.
3. You could also add tomato sauce to the cooked vegetables.
4. Heat through and spoon over hot pasta.

Wheatballs and Spaghetti

2 heaping cups cooked wheat berries (p. 4)
scant ½ cup wheat gluten powder
¼ tsp each dried dill weed and tarragon
¼ tsp each ground coriander and cumin seeds

1. Preheat oven to 350°.
2. First, use a spice mill or mortar and pestle to grind and combine the tarragon, dill, coriander, and cumin. Then purée all ingredients in a food processor. Form into about 20 medium or 30 smaller balls.
3. Place on nonstick baking sheet. Bake about 15 minutes, turn over, and bake about 15 more minutes.
4. Prepare whole wheat spaghetti and top with wheatballs and heated salsa/tomato sauce.
5. *Or*, heat baked wheatballs in a tamari- or miso-based gravy (p. 104, 136), remove from pan, place on spaghetti, and pour hot gravy over all.

BROWN RICE AND....

BASIC VEGETABLE STIR-FRY WITH RICE

1. Prepare sliced, chopped, or diced vegetables, such as turnips, rutabaga, parsnips, daikon radishes, onions, garlic, ginger root, carrots, kale, Swiss chard, cabbage, Chinese cabbage, scallions, summer squash, celery, kohlrabi, bell peppers, broccoli florets and stems, green beans, mushrooms, bok choy, edible pod peas, sea vegetables, radishes, and sprouts. Cubed tempeh or pressed tofu can also be added.
2. Sauté the vegetables in a small amount of water in the order given, so that the first cook the longest, and the last cook the least. Everything should be crisp-tender and brightly colored.
3. Serve over cooked brown rice or other grain with tamari.

Or, mix in warm rice with the last of the vegetables.

Or, include potatoes in the stir-fry (added near the top of the list) to take the place of rice.

CHOW MEIN

We call a stir-fry "chow mein" when it contains onions, celery, sliced water chestnuts, bamboo shoots, and bean and seed sprouts along with any of the other stir-fry vegetables, eaten over brown rice with tamari and hot mustard.

STEAMED VEGETABLES WITH RICE

group 1: turnips, rutabaga, parsnips, daikon radishes (15 minutes)
group 2: carrots, onions, garlic, ginger root, kale, Swiss chard (10 minutes)
group 3: scallions, summer squash, celery, kohlrabi, beans, mushrooms, green peppers, broccoli, sea vegetables (5 minutes)
group 4: peas, radishes, sprouts (1 or 2 minutes)

1. Set steamer over water and bring to a boil.
2. Place sliced vegetables from each group in the steamer for a few minutes in the order given, adding each new group on top, so the first group steams the longest and the last group steams very briefly.
3. Replace the cover after each addition of vegetables. Total steaming time should be no more than 15 minutes; everything should be crisp-tender and bright in color. Herbs can be tossed with the steamed vegetables.
4. Serve over brown rice or another grain, with tamari.

SWEET AND SOUR STIR-FRY WITH RICE

vegetables prepared for stir-fry (see p. 95)
2 tblsp tamari
2 tblsp brown rice vinegar or wine vinegar
2 tblsp rice syrup
2 tsp grated fresh, or ½ tsp dried, ginger
1 tblsp cornstarch (or arrowroot or kuzu: see p. 13)
2 tblsp water
cooked brown rice, or soba or udon noodles

1. Combine tamari, vinegar, rice syrup, and ginger.
2. Sauté vegetables in a small amount of water in a skillet until crisp-tender. Stir in tamari mixture. Mix thickener and water, add to skillet, and stir until thick.
3. Serve over rice or noodles.

"FRIED" RICE WITH VEGETABLES

ginger root, grated or finely chopped
garlic, pressed or finely chopped
tofu, pressed (p. 6) and diced, or diced tempeh
assorted chopped or diced vegetables, such as turnips, rutabaga, parsnips,
    daikon radishes, onions, green peppers, cabbage, Chinese cabbage, carrots,
    kale, Swiss chard, broccoli and cauliflower florets and stems, celery, summer
    squash, edible pod peas, sea vegetables (reconstituted by brief soaking),
    radishes, mushrooms, bok choy, kohlrabi, green beans
cooked brown rice (p. 2)
tamari
garnish – grated carrots, chopped green onions, and/or sprouts

1. Sauté ginger, garlic, and tofu in a small amount of water in a skillet or wok.
2. Add vegetables in the order given. Add rice and heat through.
3. Serve with tamari and garnishes.

Sushi Rice (Rice in Vinegar Dressing)

3 cups cooked brown rice (p. 8), still hot

Dressing:

3 tblsp brown rice vinegar   2 tsp mirin (optional)
2 tblsp rice syrup   dash tamari

1. Combine dressing ingredients. Place the rice in a large bowl.
2. Sprinkle the dressing over and mix vigorously for several minutes.
3. Let cool to room temperature.

MexiCali Rice

2 cups raw brown rice
1 cup diced onion
2 or more cloves garlic, pressed or finely chopped
3 cups chopped fresh or canned tomatoes, with 2 tsp basil and some freshly ground
     black pepper -or- 3 cups total prepared tomato sauce and/or salsa
4 cups water (with 1 tblsp vegetable broth powder, optional) or stock
½ cup each of any or all of these vegetables, chopped, diced, or sliced:
     bell pepper, carrot, mushrooms, zucchini, celery, parsley, kale,
     edible pod peas; or whole shell peas and/or corn kernels
4 oz tempeh, cut into tiny cubes (optional)

1. Soak rice in hot water 10 minutes; drain.
2. Heat a small amount of water in a skillet, add rice, and cook, stirring frequently,
   for about 5 minutes.
3. Stir in onions, garlic, and tomatoes. Cook and stir about 10 minutes.
4. Add liquid, vegetables, and tempeh. Cook, uncovered, until all the broth is
   absorbed, about 20 minutes. Reduce heat, cover, cook another 5 minutes.
5. Remove from heat, cover, and let stand 15 minutes.

DOLMADAKIAS (RICE-STUFFED GRAPE LEAVES)

4 cups chopped onions	2 tblsp lemon juice
1 cup raw brown rice	freshly ground black pepper
¼ cup chopped fresh,	½ tsp paprika
or 2 tblsp dried, parsley	1 jar grapevine leaves*
1 tsp fresh, or ½ tsp dried, dill (optional)	lemon wedges

1. Sauté onions in a small amount of water until slightly brown. Add rice and 1 cup boiling water. Cover and cook until water is absorbed. Add parsley, dill, lemon juice, pepper, and paprika. Remove from heat and let stand 5 minutes. Remove lid and cool.
2. To make rolls, wash leaves in hot water and drain. Spread a leaf on a plate wrong side up, stem toward you. Cut stem.
3. Depending on size of leaf, place 1 teaspoon to 1 tablespoon of filling near stem end, fold over sides of leaf, and roll away from you.
4. Place side by side in 2 or 3 layers in a pan lined with leaves. Pour 1½ cups boiling water over, cover, and bake in 300° oven for 1½ hours. Leave covered until cooled. Serve with lemon.
5. Chilled leftover dolmas are good on pita sandwiches (p. 70).

Grape leaves can be found in well-stocked natural foods coops and stores and in the ethnic foods section of large supermarkets.

RICE-STUFFED CABBAGE ROLLS

3 cups cooked brown rice (p. 8)	¼ cup raisins or currants
1 head green cabbage	¼ cup chopped fresh, or
1 cup chopped onions	or 2 tblsp dried, parsley
2 cups chopped mushrooms	2 tblsp dried, parsley
2 cloves garlic, pressed or finely chopped	¼ tsp nutmeg
½ cup chopped water chestnuts or	freshly ground black pepper
chopped steamed chestnuts	4 cups total tomato sauce and/or salsa

1. Steam whole cabbage until leaves are soft and translucent, then cool.
2. Meanwhile, simmer onions, mushrooms, garlic, chestnuts, and raisins in ½ cup water for 10 minutes. Remove from heat and stir in parsley, nutmeg, and pepper.
3. Stir in the cooked brown rice and 1 cup of the tomato sauce/salsa.
4. Pour another 1 cup tomato sauce/salsa over the bottom of a 9-inch square baking pan.
5. Preheat oven to 350°.
6. Remove core from cabbage and peel off whole leaves. Place ¼-½ cup filling in center of each leaf. Tuck ends under and place seam side down in baking dish. Pour remaining tomato sauce/salsa over. Cover and bake about 45 minutes.

MOCHI

Mochi is made from glutinous (sweet) brown rice which is steamed, pounded until dense, flattened, and dried. You can find it in the freezer of natural foods coops and stores. Cut the mochi slab into 6 or more smaller rectangular pieces, place on a nonstick or lightly oiled baking pan, and bake about 10 minutes in a preheated 450° oven. It will puff up like a popover, chewy on the inside and crisp on the outside. It's excellent with chutney (p. 155), corn relish (p. 152), or miso-tahini sauce (p. 136).

You can also make mochi croutons for soup or salad: Cut the mochi into small cubes (about ½ inch) and bake the same way, taking care to spread them out on the pan. Otherwise, the cubes will stick to each other and you'll have to break them apart.

Variations on the Plain Brown Rice Theme

Follow the instructions on page 2 for cooking brown rice, making these changes:

with carrots: After the rice has been cooking for about 20 minutes, stir in two cups of grated carrots (or carrot pulp from juicer) for every cup of raw rice.

with curry and vegetables: Begin cooking rice. In a small amount of water in a separate pan, for every cup of raw rice, sauté at least ½ tsp curry powder, ½ cup chopped onion, 2 pressed or finely chopped garlic cloves, and ½ cup chopped bell pepper; then add ¼ cup raisins or currants and ¾ cup water and simmer about 10 minutes. Gently combine with the rice a few minutes before the rice is done.

with curry, vegetables, and beans: To take it one step further and transform it into a dinner, add cooked lentils, adukis, kidneys, or other beans when you combine the rice and vegetables.

with onions and garlic: In a small amount of water, sauté finely chopped onion and pressed or finely chopped garlic until wilted. Add rice and water; cook.

with onions, garlic, and tomatoes: Sauté onion and garlic as above. Add diced tomatoes, a bay leaf, and freshly ground black pepper. Then add rice and water, and cook.

with onions and parsley: Sauté finely chopped onion in a small amount of water until wilted. Sprinkle on some hot sauce, then add the raw rice and water. When rice is ready, toss in finely chopped parsley.

with sea vegetables: Add 2 tblsp snipped or crumbled arame, hijiki, wakame, or other sea vegetable or combination and 1 tblsp parsley with each cup of raw rice.

OTHER GRAINS

MILLET-TOMATO CASSEROLE

3 cups cooked millet (p. 3)
2 onions, finely chopped
1 clove garlic, pressed or finely chopped
½ tsp celery seeds
2 cups total chopped canned or fresh tomatoes, tomato sauce, and/or salsa
3 tblsp chopped fresh, or 1 tsp dried, parsley
2 tblsp chopped fresh, or 1 tblsp dried, basil
½ tsp celery seeds

1. Preheat oven to 350°.
2. Combine all ingredients and spoon into a nonstick loaf pan or casserole.
3. Bake one hour, or until set.
4. If you didn't use salsa for the casserole, serve with hot sauce.

MILLET-VEGETABLE STEW

½-1 cup each chopped carrot, onion, potato, parsnip or turnip, and cabbage, and/or any other vegetables, including sea vegetables
¼ cup chopped parsley
½ cup millet
2½ cups water (with ½ tblsp vegetable broth powder, optional) or stock

Place all ingredients in a heavy pan. Bring to a boil, cover, and simmer 45 minutes.

SWEET AND SOUR MILLET AND CURRIED MILLET

See page 119.

Golabki
("Gowmbki" - Kasha-Stuffed Cabbage Rolls)

½ cup finely chopped onion
½ cup chopped mushrooms (optional)
1 cup raw buckwheat groats (kasha)
freshly ground black pepper
2 cups water
2 tblsp snipped fresh, or 1 tblsp dried, dill weed
4 oz tofu, mashed (optional)
1 small head cabbage (about 1½ lb), or half a large one
tomato sauce, salsa, or combination, with pesto or extra basil and garlic added

1. Sauté the onion (and mushrooms) in a small amount of water until tender. Add buckwheat, pepper, and water, and bring to a boil.
2. Cover and simmer 25 minutes. Stir in the dill and tofu.
3. Meanwhile, core the cabbage and steam until the leaves are soft.
4. Preheat the oven to 350°.
5. Separate the cabbage leaves and place 2-3 heaping tablespoons of the buckwheat mixture on each leaf. Roll up and tuck in the ends. Two small leaves can be used together.
6. Place rolls seam side down in a nonstick or lightly oiled 9-inch square baking dish or casserole.
7. Pour tomato sauce/salsa over to ¾ the way up the layers of rolls. (If you prefer, use water.)
8. Cover and bake 1½-2 hours, until cabbage is tender.

Kasha and Onions

cooked kasha (buckwheat groats) (p. 2)	tamari
thinly sliced onions	tahini

1. Sauté onions in a small amount of water in a large skillet until soft. There should be about the same amount of cooked kasha and onions.
2. Mix kasha into the onions, or place the kasha on a plate with the onions on top.
3. Serve with tamari and tahini, and a salad.

KASHA VARNISHKAS
(BUCKWHEAT GROATS WITH ONIONS AND PASTA)

thinly sliced or chopped onions
cooked kasha (p. 2)
cooked pasta (bow ties are traditional)

1. Sauté the onions until golden in a large skillet in a small amount of water.
2. Stir in the kasha and pasta.

Good with tamari.

Again, add a big salad, and you have dinner.

ALMOST-TRADITIONAL COUSCOUS

4 cups cooked couscous (p. 3)
1½ cups each diced carrots, onions, pumpkin, turnip or rutabaga, and zucchini
1 cup raisins or currants
1½ cups cooked chickpeas
freshly ground black pepper, cinnamon, and paprika
hot sauce and crushed cumin seed

1. Steam the diced vegetables and raisins in a large nonstick covered pot until tender, with just enough water and/or stock to keep from sticking. Add chickpeas and pepper, cinnamon, and paprika to taste.
2. Serve over couscous with hot sauce and cumin.
3. Traditional North African couscous contained lamb or chicken and was prepared in a special double steamer, with the steam from the vegetables below softening and cooking the couscous above.

Spicy Couscous

½ cup raisins, soaked in 1 cup warm water
   at least 15 minutes
½ cup chopped onion
1 clove garlic, pressed or finely chopped
2 cups boiling water
⅛ tsp each cinnamon and ground cumin

freshly ground black pepper
1½ cups couscous
1 tblsp finely chopped fresh,
   or ½ tsp dried, mint
1½ tblsp lemon juice
2 tsp balsamic vinegar

1. Sauté onion and garlic in a small amount of water (or raisin-soaking water) until wilted. Add raisins and their soaking liquid, boiling water, spices, and pepper. Bring to a boil.
2. Remove from heat and add the couscous. Stir in mint, lemon juice, and vinegar.
3. Cover and let stand 5 minutes. Uncover and fluff with a fork.

Couscous Croquettes

1 heaping cup cooked couscous (p. 3)
2 cups steamed vegetables, such as finely chopped carrots, celery, mushrooms,
   onions, summer squash; pressed or finely chopped garlic;
   snipped or crumbled sea vegetables; corn kernels, peas
4 oz tofu, mashed
dried parsley, celery seed, and basil—
   crushed in a mortar and pestle or coarsely ground in a spice mill

1. Preheat oven to 400° or preheat broiler.
2. Combine and mash all ingredients. Or, prepare vegetables in processor, then steam them and return to processor with remaining ingredients to purée.
3. Form into 8 large croquettes and place on nonstick baking sheet.
4. Bake until brown, about 30 minutes, turning once, or broil until crisp turning once.

Other Ways to Enjoy Couscous

- hot or cold, with fresh fruit and soymilk or soy yogurt (p. 10)
- just like rice pudding (heated with vanilla soy milk, rice syrup, cinnamon, raisins or currants, chopped apple and/or other fruit, and crunchy wheat and barley cereal)
- in a bowl with soup poured over it
- with steamed or sautéed vegetables
- with many of the vegetable dishes in this and the next chapter
- leftover, mixed with your morning cold or hot cereal

Wheat Berries with Soygurt and Raisins

cooked wheat berries (p. 4), well drained
raisins (or currants)
soy yogurt (p. 10)

1. Spoon wheat berries onto plate.
2. Top with raisins and yogurt.
This is a perennial favorite with pumpkin-tofu burgers (p. 122) and a salad.

Seitan - "Wheat Meat" - with Gravy

To the eye, seitan resembles pot roast when eaten with mashed potatoes and smothered in thick tamari gravy. But to the mind, body, and planet, it's a pure and nutritious food made of wheat gluten, whole wheat flour, and water.

You may find it prepared, in the freezer of a natural food coop or store, or more likely, in dry "quick mix" form in a box on the shelf. To make seitan, just follow the simple, fun directions on the box..

Tamari Gravy

½ cup water
½ cup apple juice
¼ cup tamari
1 tsp grated fresh, or ½ tsp dried, ginger
1-2 cloves garlic, pressed or finely chopped
1 tblsp cornstarch (or arrowroot or kuzu: see p. 13)
¼ cup water

1. Combine ½ cup water, juice, tamari, ginger, and garlic in a saucepan and bring to a simmer.
2. Dissolve thickener in ¼ cup water, add to simmering broth, and mix until thick.
3. For dinner, serve over prepared seitan and mashed potatoes, with a cooked vegetable and/or a big, fresh salad.

SEITAN STIR-FRY

2 cups prepared seitan, cut in strips
¼ cup tamari
1 tblsp cornstarch (or arrowroot or kuzu: see p. 13)
1 cup water (with 1 tsp vegetable broth mix, optional) or stock
2 tblsp grated fresh, or 1 tsp dried, ginger
2-3 cloves garlic, pressed or finely chopped
2 medium bell peppers, sliced
1 medium onion, thinly sliced
2 cups chopped green cabbage
1 stalk celery, chopped
2 tblsp snipped or crumbled sea vegetables
1 8-oz can unsweetened pineapple tidbits or chunks, juice reserved
cooked brown rice (p. 2)

1. Combine tamari and thickener in a medium bowl. Add seitan and toss to coat. Marinate 30 minutes. Drain, reserving sauce. Add water or stock and pineapple juice to sauce.
2. Heat a small amount of water in a large skillet. Add ginger and vegetables.
3. Stir-fry 5-8 minutes, until vegetables are crisp-tender. Add seitan and pineapple.
4. Stir-fry 2 more minutes. Add sauce and cook until it bubbles and thickens.
5. Serve over rice with a fresh, green salad.

FRUITY SAUCE FOR GRAINS AND VEGETABLES

8-oz can crushed pineapple, juice reserved
2 tblsp frozen orange juice concentrate
   (or ¼ cup orange juice, for a thinner sauce)
¼ cup apricot all-fruit preserves, or pineapricot jam (p. 204)

1. Mix drained pineapple, concentrate, and jam with a fork, or purée in a blender or processor. Add reserved pineapple juice to desired consistency. Heat.
2. Spoon over any grains, vegetables, tofu, and grain-vegetable-tofu dishes.

Sample quick dinner. Make a salad. Prepare couscous (p. 3). While couscous soaks, make the fruity sauce to spoon over it. Slice zucchini, bell peppers, onions, and mushrooms, and sauté in a small amount of water until crisp-tender. Arrange all this beautiful and delicious food on a plate for each person to enjoy.

SQUASH AND SWEET POTATOES

STUFFED ACORN SQUASH

2 acorn squash
1 cup bulgur
2 cups boiling water
1 onion, chopped
1 stalk celery and leaves, chopped
tamari

1 small carrot, diced
1 bell pepper, chopped
1-2 cloves garlic,
  pressed or finely chopped
¼ tsp each thyme and tarragon

1. Preheat oven to 400°.
2. Pour boiling water over bulgur, stir, and cover. Let stand until water is absorbed.
3. Sauté vegetables is a small amount of water. Add thyme and tarragon.
4. Cover and cook over medium-low heat for 10 minutes. Mix vegetables and bulgur and season with tamari.
5. Cut the squashes in half crosswise, scoop out seeds (to bake the seeds, see p. 212), and place squash cavity-up on a baking pan.
6. Fill cavities with stuffing and bake 45 minutes or until squash is fork-tender.

BAKED SPICED PUMPKIN OR WINTER SQUASH

1 small (4-5 pound) pumpkin or winter squash, rinsed
rice syrup (for amount, see below)
¼ tsp each cinnamon, cloves, and nutmeg
1 cup cooked light, fluffy grain, such as couscous, millet, quinoa, or rice (p. 3-4)

1. Preheat oven to 350°.
2. Cut off the top quarter of the pumpkin or squash and scoop out seeds (to bake the seeds, see p. 212). Replace lid and place in ¼ inch of water in a pie pan. Place on oven rack and bake 45-60 minutes, until just tender. The side should give slightly when pressed.
3. Scoop out pulp without piercing skin, leaving a "wall" about ½ inch thick.
4. Mash the pulp. For each cup of pulp, add 1 tblsp rice syrup. Add spices and grain and mix well. Spoon into pumpkin shell and replace lid.
5. Bake at 325° until piping hot, about 15 minutes.

Stuffed Pumpkin: A Thanksgiving Alternative

1 small (4-5 pound) pumpkin
1 cup chopped onion
1½-2 cups total whole wheat bread crumbs and/or cooked brown rice, couscous, or millet
2 tblsp soy powder
½ tsp dried sage, ground with a spice mill or a mortar and pestle
¼ tsp grated or ground nutmeg
freshly ground black pepper
8 oz tofu, mashed
1 bay leaf

1. Preheat oven to 400°.
2. Leave stem on pumpkin. Cut off top to make a lid. Remove seeds.
   (To bake the seeds, see p. 212.)
3. Sauté onions in a small amount of water. Add bread crumbs or cooked grain, soy powder, spices, and mashed tofu. Stir.
4. Place pumpkin on a pie tin. Fill with stuffing, but don't pack it in. (If there's any stuffing left over, bake it separately in a small covered casserole for about 30 minutes.) Set bay leaf on top. Pour water to within ½ inch of the top. Replace lid.
5. Bake 1½ hours, then reduce heat to 350° and bake another 30 minutes, until pumpkin is tender inside. Serve by scooping out pumpkin and stuffing together.

More-Traditional Stuffing

1 cup chopped onion
1 cup total chopped celery and mushrooms
1 cup chopped apples
½ cup chopped cranberries
1½ -2 cups total wheat bread crumbs,
   and/or cooked brown rice, couscous, or millet
2 tblsp soy powder
½ tsp thyme
freshly ground black pepper

1. Sauté onions in a small amount of water for a few minutes, followed by celery and mushrooms, then apples and cranberries.
2. Add remaining ingredients and enough water to cook and stir a few more minutes.

SQUASH IN BATTER

Batter

1 tblsp each dill seed and dill weed
1 tsp each celery seed and savory
1 tsp anise seed (optional)
1½ cups total soy grits, soy granules, and/or TVP (textured vegetable protein, p. 9)
    and wheat germ, bran, oat bran, and/or wholegrain bread crumbs
1 cup water
6 cups squash, cut into small wedges (summer: crookneck, pattypan, zucchini;
    winter: acorn, butternut, delicata)

1. Grind seeds with a spice mill or mortar and pestle to release their flavors. Combine batter ingredients. Stir in squash wedges. Refrigerate about 30 minutes.
2. Heat a small amount of water in a skillet. Add squash and batter, stir-fry a few minutes, then cover and cook over medium heat about 15 minutes, stirring occasionally, until squash is soft and batter is crisp.
3. This is great with a fresh salad, as a meal, or even mixed right in with the salad and some brown rice vinegar or wine vinegar on your dinner plate.

SUCCHINI SUEY WITH SALSA, SOUTHERN STYLE

sliced zucchini, onions, mushrooms, and celery
salsa or a mix of salsa and tomato sauce
cooked corn grits (p. 23)

1. Steam vegetables or sauté in a small amount of water.
2. Serve over cooked grits, topped with salsa/tomato sauce.
Particularly good on the tailgate after a day of hiking in Shenandoah National Park.

MILLET-WINTER SQUASH STEW

½ cup chopped onion
1-2 cloves garlic, pressed or finely chopped
2 generous cups peeled winter squash
    in ½-inch cubes (butternut is easiest to peel)

1 cup millet
3½ cups water
1 tblsp tamari

1. Sauté onion and garlic in a small amount of water. Add squash, millet, water, and tamari. Bring to a boil, cover, and simmer 25-30 minutes, until water is absorbed. Let stand 10 minutes before serving.
2. For a deep-sea flavor, sauté snipped or crumbled sea vegetables with the onion and garlic, stir in with the squash, or toss in as a garnish.

DOUBLE SWEET POTATO CASSEROLE

3 cups sliced sweet potatoes
2 cups peeled, cored, and sliced apples
1 cup thinly sliced carrots
1 cup thinly sliced sweet onions
½ cup thinly sliced bell peppers
1 20-oz can crushed pineapple or tidbits, drained
4 cups cooked couscous, millet, or quinoa (p. 3-4)
  (For a triple-sweet casserole, cook the grain in apple juice.)

1. Preheat oven to 375°.
2. The apples and vegetables can be prepared in an instant using the slicing disc of a food processor. Steam sweet potatoes, apples, carrots, and onions over boiling water until crisp-tender. Add peppers.
3. Make layers in a large nonstick or lightly oiled casserole: ⅓ of the cooked grain, half the steamed mixture, and half the drained pineapple. Repeat, and finally top with remaining grain. Pour drained pineapple juice over.
4. Bake about 30 minutes. Add a big salad; there's dinner.

Note: For a simpler version of a similar dinner, steam cubed or sliced sweet potatoes and serve with a cooked grain, warmed pineapple (you can add cranberries and diced apples as it heats), and a green salad.

OTHER VEGETABLE MAIN DISHES

TANGY SIMMERED MARINATED VEGETABLES

Marinade

½ cup brown rice vinegar
  or red wine vinegar
½ cup water
2 tsp tamari
2 cloves garlic, pressed or finely chopped
1 tblsp grated fresh,
  or ½ tsp dried, ginger
3 tblsp frozen orange
  or apple juice concentrate
¼ cup pineapple tidbits
¼ cup pineapple juice, drained from tidbits
a few shakes hot sauce

Vegetables

1 cup sliced summer squash
1 small bell pepper (red if available),
  seeded and slivered
½ cup thinly sliced carrots
2 cups cauliflower florets
½ cup sliced mushrooms
1 thinly sliced broccoli stem
¼ cup sliced water chestnuts
2 tblsp snipped or crumbled sea
  vegetables (optional)

1. Combine marinade ingredients in a saucepan. Add the vegetables and simmer about 10 minutes.
2. Serve over a cooked grain, such as brown rice or couscous. The artistic mix of color on the plate matches the flavorful blend of tastes on the palette.

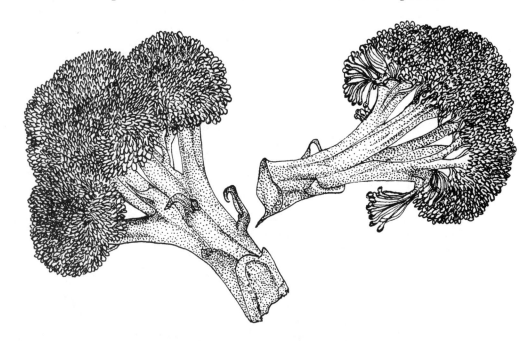

Late-Summer Stew

3-4 cups quartered and sliced potatoes
5-6 cups chunked eggplant
florets and chopped tender stems from 1 head cauliflower
2-3 cups chopped onion
2 or more cloves garlic, pressed or finely chopped
2 tblsp snipped or crumbled sea vegetables (optional)
1½ tsp ground cumin
1 bay leaf
\about 6 fresh or canned tomatoes, coarsely chopped
1 tblsp grated fresh, or ¾ tsp dried, ginger
½ cup chopped fresh, or 2 tblsp dried, parsley
soy yogurt (p. 10) (optional)

1. Set up a steamer in a large pot. Steam potatoes 10 minutes; and eggplant and steam 5 minutes; add cauliflower and steam until everything is just soft.
2. Meanwhile, sauté onions, garlic (and sea vegetables) in a small amount of water for 1 or 2 minutes, then add cumin and bay leaf and continue to sauté until onions begin to brown.
3. Add tomatoes and ginger, and the steamed vegetables.
4. Serve with parsley and soy yogurt.

Harvest Stew

Any or all of these vegetables:

onions, cut into wedges
garlic, pressed or finely chopped
bell peppers, cut into large pieces
summer squash, sliced into
    thick half- or quarter-rounds
mushrooms, thickly sliced
celery, sliced
corn kernels scraped from ears of corn

tomatoes, cut into sections
florets and sliced stems from
    broccoli or cauliflower
eggplant, cut into chunks
carrots, thickly sliced
sea vegetables, snipped or crumbled
crushed herbs: basil, cumin, tarragon, thyme
¾ cup V-8 juice, tomato juice, or
    tomato sauce (p. 90)

1. Sauté onion and garlic in a small amount of water until wilted.
2. Add other vegetables, herbs, and V-8 juice or tomato sauce.
3. Cover and simmer about 20 minutes.
4. Serve over a cooked whole grain or pasta.

Ratatouille (Eggplant-Tomato Stew)

2 cups sliced onions
2 or more cloves garlic, pressed or finely chopped
1 large eggplant, peeled and cut into ½ inch cubes
2-3 small zucchini, sliced into half-rounds
1 diced bell pepper
1 tsp-1 tblsp paprika
freshly ground black pepper
1 28-oz can tomatoes, chopped, or 4 cups chopped fresh tomatoes
1 tsp dried oregano and/or other herbs: basil, marjoram, parsley, savory, thyme
cooked brown rice, millet, or orzo

1. In a large skillet, sauté the onions and garlic in a small amount of water until soft. Add the eggplant, zucchini, and bell pepper, and cook 5 minutes.
2. Sprinkle with paprika and pepper and cook 1 minute.
3. Add the tomatoes, their juice, and the herbs.
4. Bring to a boil, cover, and simmer until the eggplant is tender.
5. Serve over brown rice, millet, orzo, or another grain.

Dutch Oven Vegetables

4 peeled onions	2 cups whole mushrooms
4 medium zucchini	2 bell peppers, seeded and cut in large pieces
4 carrots	1 tsp ground cumin*

1. Preheat oven to 350°.
2. The onions, zucchini, and carrots can be left whole or cut into 2 or 3 pieces. Place vegetables in a large nonstick or lightly oiled casserole. Sprinkle cumin on top. Cover and bake one hour. Serve with a cooked whole grain or orzo, and some kind of sauce (check index for ideas).
3. *Or crush the whole seeds in a spice mill or with a mortar and pestle.

Shepherd's Pie

1. Preheat oven to 375°.
2. Line a nonstick or lightly oiled pie tin with mashed potatoes (p. 157).
3. Fill with very lightly steamed vegetables.
4. Top with more mashed potatoes. Bake until piping hot.
5. Serve with hot sauce and/or freshly ground black pepper.

PARSNIP PIE

Crust*
¾ cup rolled oats
¼ cup whole wheat pastry flour
¼ cup brown rice flour
6-8 tblsp (⅓-½ cup water)

Filling
6 cups sliced parsnips, steamed until tender
1-2 tblsp tahini

1. Preheat the oven to 350°.
2. For the crust, combine the oats and flours. Stir in enough water to make a slightly moist dough. Pat into a nonstick or lightly oiled 9-inch pie pan to form a pie shell. Bake 5-10 minutes.
3. For the filling, mash the parsnips and stir in the tahini, or blend in a food processor. Fill crust and bake 30 minutes.

*Or use millet crust, p. 193.

PARSNIP AND CARROT PIE

Steam a total of 6 sliced parsnips and carrots.

Or, for another pretty pie, steam and purée carrots and parsnips separately and arrange them in layers in the pie shell.

RUTABURGERS

1 softball-sized rutabaga, peeled
1 large carrot
1 medium onion
¾ pound tofu, pressed (p. 6), or
   ¾ cup TVP (p. 9), soaked in ⅔ cup water
¼ cup bran (optional)

¾ cup quick oats
⅛ tsp celery seeds
¼ tsp dill weed
¼ tsp thyme, crushed
¼ tsp tarragon, crushed
freshly ground black pepper

1. Finely grate the rutabaga and the carrot, grate the onion, and mix the grated vegetables in a large bowl. In a small bowl, mash the pressed tofu with a fork. Add tofu or soaked TVP to the grated vegetables along with the bran, oats and herbs. Mix well.
2. Or, put the rutabaga, carrot, and onion through the grating disk of a food processor, and then chop with the metal blade. Mix the rest of the ingredients with the vegetables in the processor.
3. Form into 12-14 small or 6-8 large burgers. Grill outside, or broil, turning when brown on one side, or bake at 400°, turning when brown on the bottom, about 15 minutes on each side.
4. Serve small rutaburgers in pita pockets. Stuff pita halves with greens, alfalfa sprouts, sliced mushrooms, 2 rutaburgers, and salsa. Or omit salsa and spread miso on one side of the pita and tahini on the other.
5. Serve large rutaburgers on whole wheat bread, toast, or buns with lettuce, sprouts, sliced onions, mushrooms, tomatoes, and your choice of sauce.

Rutaburgers can be prepared in advance and frozen.

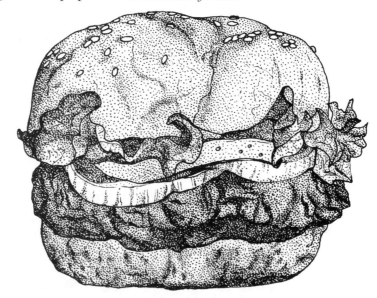

STUFFED MUSHROOMS

10-20 mushroom caps—enough to line the bottom of a 9-inch round baking pan
2 cups total chopped mushroom stems, onions, celery, parsley, sea vegetables
1½ cups cooked couscous (p. 3)
½-¾ cup chopped steamed chestnuts (p. 213) or canned sliced water chestnuts
¼ tsp each dried dill weed, tarragon, and thyme
¼ tsp each cumin and coriander seeds
freshly ground black pepper

1. Steam mushroom caps until just beginning to soften. Place in nonstick or lightly oiled baking pan.
2. Preheat oven to 350°.
3. Briefly sauté vegetables in a small amount of water.
4. Grind herbs and spices with a spice mill or mortar and pestle; combine with vegetables. Stir in cooked couscous and chopped chestnuts.
5. Spoon stuffing over caps, pat down lightly, and bake about 30 minutes.
6. You can use another stuffing, such as for pumpkin (p. 107) or acorn squash (p. 106).

STUFFED PEPPERS I

bell peppers
cooked grain, such as barley, bulgur, couscous, millet, quinoa, or rice (p. 3-4)
sautéed vegetables: chopped or sliced carrots, celery, green beans, mushrooms, onions, parsley, spinach; corn; pressed or finely chopped garlic; snipped or crumbled sea vegetables; others
oregano, basil, and/or other dried herbs
salsa, tomato sauce, or combination

1. Slice the tops off the peppers and remove the seeds. Place upside-down in a steamer over boiling water and steam until just tender, about 5-10 minutes. Steam the tops, too.
2. Preheat oven to 350°.
3. Combine the cooked grain, sautéed vegetables, and herbs. Add stock or water if it's too dry. Fill the steamed peppers and place upright in a baking pan. Pour salsa/tomato sauce over all. Replace tops or place them alongside the stuffed peppers. Cover the pan and bake until piping hot—about 20-30 minutes.
4. Any extra stuffing is ready to eat, or you can bake it in a nonstick or lightly oiled baking pan.

STUFFED PEPPERS II

1. Omit the herbs and salsa/tomato sauce. Instead, combine grated fresh ginger root, cayenne, and tamari with the sautéed vegetables.
2. Pour about ½ inch of stock or water into the pan before covering and baking.
3. Other stuffings can be used as well.

SWEET CABBAGE ROLLS

1 head cabbage, steamed whole until leaves are soft and translucent, then cooled
3-4 cups cooked amaranth, brown rice, millet, couscous, quinoa,
   or other sweet grain (p. 3-4)
4-5 sweet potatoes, chunked, steamed, and mashed
¾ cup chopped onion, water-sautéed (optional)
1 8-oz can unsweetened crushed pineapple
1 cup raisins or currants (can be plumped in water or fruit juice in advance)
1½ cups chopped apples
1½ tsp cinnamon
Fruity Sauce for Grains and Vegetables (p. 105)

1. In a bowl, combine 1 cup cooked grain with remaining filling ingredients: sweet potatoes, onion, pineapple, raisins, apples, and cinnamon.
2. Pour half of the Fruity Sauce over the bottom of a 9-inch square baking pan.
3. Preheat oven to 375°.
4. Remove core from cabbage and peel off whole leaves. Place ¼ - ½ cup filling in center of each leaf. Tuck ends under and place seam side down in baking dish. Pour remaining sauce over.
5. Cover and bake about 30 minutes.

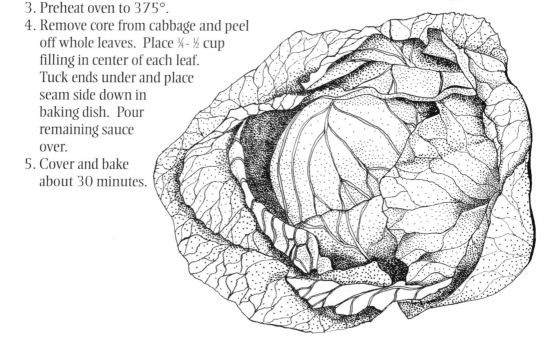

BEANS

FALAFEL

2 large onions	1 tsp cumin seeds
4 cups cooked (p. 5)	½ tsp each basil, oregano, and thyme
or canned chickpeas	2 tblsp tamari
2 tblsp caraway seeds	2 tblsp chopped fresh, or
2 tblsp curry powder	1 tblsp dried, parsley
1 tblsp paprika	½ cup whole wheat flour or quick oats
boiling water	

1. Chop the onions in a food processor, then blend with remaining ingredients plus just enough boiling water so you can form the mixture into ping-pong size balls.
2. Place the falafel balls on a non-stick or lightly oiled baking pan.
3. Bake at 350° until nicely browned, about 30 minutes, turning once or twice.

Falafel Sauce

½ cup tahini	1 tsp ground cumin
¼ cup lemon or lime juice	2 or more cloves garlic,
2 tblsp tamari	pressed or finely chopped

1. Mix well, then add water to desired thinness.
2. To assemble: Cut pita in half and line with lettuce or other greens, sprouts, and sliced tomatoes.
3. Place falafel balls inside and pour sauce over all.

CHICKPEA STEW

1½ cups finely chopped onions
4 cups cooked (or canned) chickpeas (p. 5), drained
2 large tomatoes, chopped
1 6-oz can tomato paste
1 cup water
1 tsp each ground coriander and cumin
  (or whole seeds crushed in a spice mill or with a mortar and pestle)
1 tsp ground cumin*
¼ tsp ground turmeric
2 tblsp chopped fresh, or 1 tblsp dried, parsley
2 tblsp chopped fresh, or 2 tsp dried, basil

1. Sauté the onions in a small amount of water until wilted.
2. Add the chickpeas, tomatoes, tomato paste, water, coriander, cumin, and turmeric.
3. Cover and simmer 30 minutes.
4. Sprinkle with parsley and basil.

CHICKPEA AND VEGETABLE STEW WITH MILLET

1½ cups chopped onion
2 tblsp snipped or crumbled sea vegetables (optional)
3 cups chopped mushrooms
3 tblsp lemon juice
2 cups cooked (or canned) chickpeas (p. 5), drained
½ tsp paprika
freshly ground black pepper
dash cayenne
chopped florets and stems from 1 head fresh broccoli
4 cups cooked millet (p. 3)

1. Sauté onion (and sea vegetables) in a small amount of water until soft. Add mushrooms and sauté a few more minutes.
2. Stir in lemon juice, chickpeas, paprika, pepper, and cayenne, and heat through.
3. Add broccoli and cook briefly, only until the broccoli is bright green and crisp-tender.
4. Serve over cooked millet.

SWEET AND SOUR LENTILS OR MILLET

Combine in a saucepan and heat thoroughly:

2-2½ cups cooked lentils (p. 5) or millet (p. 3)
1-2 cloves garlic, pressed or finely chopped
2 tblsp rice syrup
2 tblsp balsamic, brown rice, cider, or wine vinegar
dash of nutmeg or cloves

CURRIED LENTILS OR MILLET

Replace spice, rice syrup, and vinegar with ½ cup finely chopped onion, 1 tsp curry powder, and a small amount of water.

VEGETABLE-AND-BEAN CURRY

¾ tsp each ground cumin and coriander*	1½ cups thinly sliced onions
1½ tblsp curry powder	2 cups small cauliflower florets
¼ tsp cayenne	and sliced stems
½ tsp mild to hot chili powder (optional)	1½ cups thinly sliced zucchini
⅛ tsp each cardamom, cloves,	1½ cups total chopped fresh or
and cinnamon (optional)	canned tomatoes and/or salsa
freshly ground black pepper	1½ cups cooked chickpeas, lentils,
2 cloves garlic, pressed or finely chopped	or diced tempeh
1 cup water or vegetable stock	½ cup raisins or currants
1½ cups thinly sliced carrots	cooked brown rice
1½ cups diced peeled potatoes	soy yogurt (optional)
1 cup thinly sliced bell pepper	

1. Water-sauté the spices and garlic for a few minutes, then stir in the water or stock and cook for 2 minutes.
2. Add the carrots, potatoes, pepper, onions, and cauliflower. Cover and simmer until the vegetables are just tender, about 5-7 minutes.
3. Add zucchini, tomatoes/salsa, beans or tempeh, and raisins, and more water or stock if needed. Cover and simmer about 10 minutes.
4. Serve over rice, with soy yogurt.

Or crush the whole seeds in a spice mill or with a mortar and pestle.

Note: Other vegetables, such as green or wax beans, cabbage, celery, kale or other greens, kohlrabi, mushrooms, parsley, parsnips, or peas (add at the last minute) can be added or substituted.

Lentil Loaf

2 cups cooked lentils (p. 5)
1 cup cooked plain oatmeal (p. 22) or cooked brown rice (p. 2)
¼ cup soy grits or soy granules
½ cup water (with 1 tsp vegetable broth mix, optional), or stock
½ cup finely chopped onion
2 tblsp chopped fresh, or 1 tblsp dried, parsley
¼ tsp tarragon

1. Preheat the oven to 375°.
2. Combine the lentils and oatmeal or rice.
3. Soak the soy grits in the water or stock 5 minutes. Add to lentil mixture.
4. Add remaining ingredients and mix well.
5. Transfer to a nonstick or lightly oiled loaf pan.
6. Bake about 45 minutes.

Sliced lentil loaf is good with salsa/tomato sauce or a tamari- or miso-based sauce (p. 104). Leftovers make great sandwiches (see p. 70).

Lentil-Grain Burgers

2 cups cooked lentils - or any legume (p. 5)
1 cup cooked light, fluffy grain, such as couscous, millet, or quinoa (p. 3-4)
½ cup finely chopped onion
1 cup grated carrot
freshly ground black pepper
½ tsp celery seeds
4 oz tofu, mashed (optional)
sandwich ingredients (see below)

1. Preheat oven to 350°.
2. Mash well by hand or combine in a food processor the lentils or other beans, grain, onion, pepper, celery seeds, and tofu.
3. Form into burgers and bake on a nonstick baking sheet about 30 minutes, turning after 20 minutes.
4. Serve in pita pockets with sprouts, greens, sliced onions and mushrooms, and salsa; or as a whole wheat bread sandwich: miso on one slice, tahini on the other, plus sprouts, greens, and sliced onions, mushrooms, and tomatoes.

Curried Lentils and Vegetables with Rice

2 cups cooked green or red lentils*
1½ cups chopped onion
2 cloves garlic, pressed or finely chopped
1½ tsp ground cumin
1 tsp turmeric
¼ tsp dried mustard
1 tblsp grated fresh ginger
½ cup water or stock
1 cup total diced fresh or canned tomatoes, tomato sauce, and/or salsa
2 tblsp lemon juice
2 cups cut-up vegetables: broccoli, cauliflower, Brussels sprouts, green beans,
    summer squash, and/or others
cooked brown rice

1. Sauté onion and garlic in a small amount of water until onion starts to brown.
2. Stir in spice and cook briefly. Blend in water or stock, tomatoes, and lemon juice.
3. Add vegetables, stir to mix, then cover and simmer until vegetables are crisp-
    tender. Stir in lentils and heat through.
4. Serve over brown rice.

Cubed tempeh—raw, baked, or broiled—can be substituted for the lentils.

Tejas Rice and Beans

1 cup total diced onions and/or scallions
2 or more cloves garlic, pressed or finely chopped
½ cup each of any or all of these vegetables, chopped, diced, or sliced:
    bell pepper, carrot, celery, mushrooms, parsley, zucchini
2 tblsp sea vegetables (optional)
3 cups chopped fresh or canned tomatoes, with 2 tsp total basil, oregano,
    and/or thyme and some freshly ground black pepper,
    or 3 cups total prepared tomato sauce and/or salsa
1½ cups cooked black, kidney, or pinto beans (p. 5); or one 15-oz can, drained;
    or 1 package tempeh, cubed
4 cups cooked brown rice (p. 2)
other seasonings: ½ tsp paprika, ⅛ tsp cayenne, 1 tsp vinegar (optional)

Sauté vegetables in a small amount of water until tender. Stir in tomatoes, beans,
    rice, and seasonings. Heat. If you didn't use salsa, you can serve with hot sauce.
Or, combine vegetables and beans or tempeh, heat through and serve over or
    beside the rice. Either way, be sure to have fresh salad along with it.

Sweet and Sour Rice and Beans

4 cups cooked brown rice, cooled (p. 2)
1 cup cooked (or canned) kidney beans,
  drained (p. 5; cook extra for other uses)
1 cup corn kernels or diced celery
¼ cup diced bell pepper (red looks nicest)
¼ cup diced onions or scallions
¼ cup fresh, or 2 tblsp dried, parsley

1 tsp chili powder
1 tsp ground cumin
¼ cup rice syrup (may be
  thinned with hot water)
⅜ cup lime juice
hot sauce

1. Mix rice, beans, and vegetables. Combine chili, cumin, rice syrup, and lime juice.
2. Toss with the rice mixture. Serve with dashes of hot sauce.

Black Bean Enchiladas

2 medium onions, finely chopped
2-4 cloves garlic,
  pressed or finely chopped (optional)
1 tsp ground cumin (optional)

4 cups cooked black beans (p. 5)
16 small corn tortillas
2 cups salsa

1. Preheat oven to 350°.
2. Sauté the onion, garlic, and
   cumin in a small amount of
   water until tender. Mash
   or purée with the beans.
   (When this mixture is
   cooked, it's called
   refried beans.)
3. Heat the salsa.
   Simmer each tortilla in
   the salsa until just soft.
   (Don't overcook—the
   tortilla will begin to
   disintegrate.) Lay the
   tortilla flat on a plate.
   Place ¼ cup bean mixture on the
   tortilla and roll it up. Place seam side down
   in a baking pan. When all tortillas are filled,
   pour any extra salsa over the top.
4. Bake, covered, until heated through,
   about 20 minutes.

Sweet Aduki Bean Pie

1 instant pressed crust (p. 191) or millet crust (p. 193)
2½-3 cups chopped apples
1½ cups raisins
1 tblsp grated lemon or lime rind, 2 tblsp lemon or lime juice, or combination
½ tsp cinnamon
¼ tsp cloves
¼ tsp nutmeg
1 heaping tsp dry instant grain beverage (p. 217)
¾ cup boiling water
1½-2 cups cooked or canned aduki beans (p. 5)

1. Preheat oven to 350°.
2. Bake crust alone for 15 minutes.
3. Meanwhile, in a large pan, combine apples, raisins, rind and/or juice, spices, grain beverage, and water. Bring to a simmer, then cover and cook over low heat for 15-20 minutes.
4. Add beans, mix well, and cook 5 minutes. (If needed, uncover and cook a few more minutes to boil off any remaining liquid.)
5. Add filling to crust and bake 15-20 minutes.

Though this replaces mincemeat pie at Thanksgiving, you'll want to have it more than once a year!

TVP Chili

4 cups total salsa and/or tomato sauce	1½ tsp cumin seed, ground in a spice mill
1½ cups diced mushrooms	or with a mortar and pestle
½-1 cup diced bell peppers	1 tsp oregano
1 cup chopped onion	½ tsp allspice
2-4 cloves garlic, pressed or finely chopped	1 cup TVP (textured vegetable protein,
other chopped vegetables, such as	p. 9)
celery and carrots	2 tblsp chopped sea vegetables (optional)
	¼ cup tamari (optional)

1. Combine all ingredients in a large pan. Cover and bring to a boil, stirring frequently. Add water if it's too thick. Reduce heat and simmer at least ½ hour, stirring occasionally and adding water if needed.
2. Serve immediately over rice or another whole grain with a salad.

Or, give the flavors a chance to meld by refrigerating overnight and reheat the next day.

Dahl (Curried Beans)

3 cups cooked small beans, such as mung (see below),
  aduki (p. 5), or red or green lentils (p. 5)
1 tsp each ground turmeric and cayenne
2 tsp ground cumin
3 tsp ground coriander
¼ tsp dried mustard
1 tblsp grated fresh, or ½ tsp dried, ginger
I cup sliced onion
2 or more cloves garlic, pressed or finely chopped
1 cup sliced mushrooms
chopped bell pepper and tomato (optional)
1 tblsp lemon juice (optional)
1 tblsp chopped fresh, or 1 tsp dried, parsley or cilantro (optional)

1. To cook mung beans, soak 1 cup of dry beans overnight in plenty of water, drain, and rinse. Return to saucepan and cover with water.
2. Cover the pot, bring to a boil, and simmer 45-60 minutes, until the beans are very soft. To prevent boiling over, keep the lid slightly open. Add boiling water if necessary.
3. When beans are almost ready, sauté spices in a small amount of water until brown. Add the onion and garlic and sauté until brown, then add the mushrooms, bell pepper, and tomato.
4. Stir-fry everything for 10-15 minutes, until well-browned, actually dark.
5. Combine with beans and add hot boiled water to desired thinness. Cook uncovered 5-10 minutes. Stir in lemon juice and parsley. Serve over rice or as a dip or sauce.

Gingery Beans

Prepare 5 cups cooked beans (p. 5), singly or in combination, such as aduki, black, kidney, lima, navy, and/or pinto.

1 cup chopped onion	1 tblsp dried parsley
2 cups chopped fresh	1½ tsp dry mustard
or canned tomatoes	3 tblsp grated fresh,
2 tblsp rice syrup	or 1¼ tsp dried, ginger
1 tblsp vinegar	½ tsp cinnamon
1 tblsp tamari	freshly ground black pepper

1. Simmer onion for 10 minutes in a small amount of water in a large covered pot.
2. Add everything else except the beans, and cook and stir for 5 minutes.
3. Add beans and cook another 10-15 minutes. Serve over rice with a fresh salad.

BAKED BEANS

1 cup dry beans, such as navy or pinto
3 cups water
2 onions, quartered
other cut-up vegetables, such as carrots, celery, bell pepper, or parsley (optional)
¼ cup apple butter (p. 204), rice syrup, or barley malt syrup
2 tblsp tamari
grated fresh or dried ginger (optional)
dried mustard (optional)

1. Soak beans in water overnight or boil 1 minute and soak 2 hours.
2. Preheat oven to 325°.
3. Put beans, soaking water, onions, and other vegetables in a covered bean pot or other ceramic casserole.
4. Bake 1½ hours or more, until completely tender.
5. Add sweetener, tamari, and spices, and mix.
6. Bake another half hour, adding more water if needed.

Energy-saving alternative to baked beans: Follow the recipe for baked beans, except simmer in a covered pot on stovetop.

BURRITOS

cooked brown rice
cooked or canned kidney beans or other beans
salsa or a mixture of salsa and tomato sauce
whole wheat pita
greens
chopped onions
fluffy sprouts, such as alfalfa and red clover

1. Heat separately the rice, beans, and salsa/tomato sauce. (The beans, or beans with salsa/tomato sauce, can also be mashed by hand or combined in a food processor.)
2. Heat or toast the pita until soft and warm, and cut in half to make pockets.
3. Line the pockets with greens as a nest for the rice, well-drained beans, salsa, onions, and sprouts.

TOFU

Any tofu or tempeh and vegetable dish served with a cooked grain or wholegrain bread and a large, fresh green salad, makes a delicious, nutritious, and filling dinner.

TOFU AND BROCCOLI

8 oz tofu	3 tblsp tamari
1 head fresh broccoli	2 tblsp water
3 or more cloves garlic,	dash cayenne
pressed or finely chopped	lemon wedges

1. Cut tofu into ½-inch slices, and press (p. 6).
2. Cut off broccoli florets, and thinly slice all but the toughest part of the stems.
3. Cut pressed tofu into cubes. Sauté cubes in a small amount of water or sesame oil, turning frequently. Remove tofu from pan. Briefly sauté broccoli florets, sliced broccoli stems, and garlic in a small amount of water until broccoli is bright green. Sprinkle on tamari, water, and cayenne, toss with the tofu, cover, and lower heat. Cook about 3 minutes, until broccoli is crisp-tender.
4. Serve, with lemon, as soon as possible, or the broccoli will wilt and lose its bright color and flavor. Good with a salad and rice or baked or mashed potatoes.

CURRIED TOFU AND BROCCOLI

2 cups thinly sliced onions
1½ cups sliced mushrooms
3 cups small broccoli florets and sliced stems
1-2 tsp curry powder
1 tblsp grated fresh, or ¾ tsp dried, ginger
1 cup water (with 1 tsp vegetable broth powder, optional) or stock
1 tblsp tamari
1 tblsp cornstarch (or arrowroot or kuzu: see p. 13)
¼ cup water
8 oz firm tofu, diced
tomatoes - cut in quarters, eighths, or sixteenths, depending on size

1. Sauté the onions in a small amount of water until tender. Add the mushrooms and broccoli and stir-fry 3 minutes.
2. Sprinkle with the curry powder and ginger. Gradually stir in the broth and bring to a boil. Cover and cook 2-3 minutes, or until the vegetables are crisp-tender.
3. Mix tamari, thickener, and water. Add to the skillet and cook, stirring, until the mixture thickens. Add the tofu and reheat. Add the tomatoes and toss.

Quinoa-Tofu Loaf

2 cups cooked quinoa (p. 4) or other grain
1 cup chopped onion
2 or more cloves garlic, pressed or finely chopped
8 oz tofu, pressed (p. 6) and cubed, or 8 oz grated tempeh
freshly ground black pepper
marjoram, tarragon, and/or savory to taste
anise, celery, or flax seeds to taste
1 cup whole grain bread crumbs,
   or TVP (textured vegetable protein, p. 9) softened in ¾ cup water
1 cup fresh soymilk (p. 9) or ¼ cup soy powder with 1 cup water
corn and/or peas (optional)

1. Preheat oven to 350°.
2. Sauté onion and garlic in a small amount of water in a large pan. Add cooked quinoa; stir for 2 minutes. Add cubed tofu; stir for 2 minutes. Stir in pepper, herbs, seeds, and bread crumbs or softened TVP, soymilk or soy powder and water, and corn and/or peas.
3. Place mixture in a nonstick or lightly oiled loaf pan.
4. Cover and bake 20 minutes. Remove cover and bake another 10 minutes, until nicely browned.

Eggplant Parmigiana

brown rice, cooked
eggplant: peeled, sliced lengthwise, and steamed
tofu, mashed
salsa or a mix of salsa and tomato sauce
oregano
freshly ground black pepper

1. Preheat oven to 375°.
2. Place half the brown rice in a nonstick or lightly oiled casserole. Top with half the eggplant, then half the tofu, cover with salsa/tomato sauce, and sprinkle with oregano and pepper. Repeat the layers.
3. Cover and bake about 30 minutes, until piping hot.

Note: You can use zucchini instead of eggplant. It's a good way to make use of one of those giant zucchinis you find hidden in the garden.

Or, if you find yourself living in a tropical locale, substitute breadfruit for the eggplant.

TOFU LASAGNA

12 oz tofu, sliced and pressed (p. 6)
½ cup chopped onion
3 cloves garlic, pressed or finely chopped
⅛ tsp nutmeg
2 tblsp dried parsley
12 cooked whole wheat lasagna noodles*
2 cups chopped greens, such as spinach, kale, Chinese cabbage, chard, broccoli
about 4 cups total salsa and/or tomato sauce

1. Preheat oven to 375°.
2. Mash the pressed tofu and combine with the onion, garlic, nutmeg, and parsley.
3. Steam the greens briefly, until just wilted and bright green . If you use broccoli, steam the other vegetables a few minutes before adding it to the steamer.
4. In a nonstick or lightly oiled baking pan, layer half the cooked noodles, half the steamed vegetables, half the tofu mixture, and salsa/tomato sauce to cover. Repeat the layers.
5. Bake about 45 minutes, until piping hot. Cover the pan after about 25 minutes.
Other wholegrain pasta can be used in place of lasagna noodles.

VEGETABLE-TOFU CASSEROLE

Part 1: Choose one of these vegetable combinations, or prepare one of your own. Sauté vegetables in a small amount of water until crisp-tender. Remove from pan.

1 eggplant, peeled and cubed, and several zucchini, sliced into ¼ inch rounds; or florets from 1 head broccoli or cauliflower, 1 diced red pepper, and 1 cup peas; or 6-8 cups torn or chopped spinach, kale, or Swiss chard, and 1 cup sliced mushrooms

Part 2:

3 ribs celery, chopped	3 bay leaves
2 onions, chopped	¼ cup red wine vinegar
3 cloves garlic, pressed or finely chopped	½ cup tamari
8 oz tofu, cut into ½-inch slices, pressed, then cut into cubes	

1. In the same pan, sauté celery, onions, garlic, and tofu in a small amount of water until onions are transparent. Combine with the other vegetables and place in a nonstick or lightly oiled casserole. Place bay leaves here and there as it's being filled. Pour wine vinegar and tamari over.
2. Cover and bake at 325° until piping hot.
3. Serve with or over brown rice or other whole grain.

Tofu Loaf, Burgers, or Casserole

8 oz tofu
1 or 2 onions, finely chopped
2 or more cloves garlic, pressed or finely chopped
¼ cup fresh, or 2 tblsp dried, parsley
1 or more cups other vegetables, chopped and briefly steamed
2-4 tblsp miso, thinned in a few tblsp warm water, or ¼ cup tamari
½ cup cooked grain, such as brown rice, bulgur, or millet; or cooked chickpeas,
    mashed or ground in a processor; or whole wheat bread crumbs
other dried herbs, such as celery seed, dill seed, tarragon, or thyme.
    (Basil goes well with tomatoes.)

1. Preheat oven to 350°.
2 Mash or blend all ingredients together. Place in nonstick or lightly oiled loaf
   pan or form into burgers and place on nonstick or lightly oiled baking sheet.
3. Bake 45-60 minutes, until brown and firm. Flip burgers after about 20 minutes.
4. Cool loaf slightly, remove from pan and slice thickly.
5. Place burger or loaf slice on plate, top or serve with brown rice and steamed or
   stir-fried vegetables (p. 95) or "fried" rice (p. 96).

Or eat burgers or sliced loaf as a sandwich on whole wheat bread or pita with
   sliced onions, tomatoes, mushrooms, fluffy sprouts (alfalfa and red clover)
   and miso/tahini or salsa.

Or make a casserole: cooked brown rice on the bottom, then a layer of lightly
   steamed or stir-fried vegetables, topped with the tofu casserole-burger mix.
   If you like, pour tomato sauce and/or salsa over. Bake 45-60 minutes.
   Add a fresh salad to make a meal.

Basic Dark Green Leafy-Tofu Pie

9-inch pie crust (p. 191-192)
½-1 cup sliced or chopped onions
2-3 quarts torn, rinsed spinach, kale, or Swiss chard leaves
4-8 oz tofu, mashed

1. Preheat oven to 375°.
2. Sauté onions briefly in a small amount of water.
3. Add leaves (no need to add more water, only what clings to the rinsed leaves),
   cover, and cook over medium-low heat just until wilted.
4. Place in crust. Top with mashed tofu.
5. Bake about 30 minutes, until piping hot.
Good with hot sauce.

Spinach, Mushroom, and Tofu Pie

9-inch pie crust (p. 191-192) baked at 400° for 10 minutes

Filling:

4 cups rinsed, torn or coarsely chopped spinach, kale, or Swiss chard leaves	5-6 cups sliced mushrooms
	1 bunch parsley, chopped
2-3 cloves garlic, pressed or finely chopped	½ cup chopped onions

Sauté vegetables in a small amount of water for 5 minutes. Place in baked pie crust.

Topping:

12 oz tofu (silken makes it very creamy)	¼ tsp dry mustard
3 tblsp each red wine vinegar and tamari	freshly ground black pepper

1. Purée topping ingredients in a blender or processor.
2. Spoon over vegetables in pie crust and bake 20 minutes at 350°.

Vegetable-Tofu Pie

9-inch pie crust (p. 191-192) baked at 400° for 10 minutes

Filling:	*Topping:*
3 carrots, diced	12 oz tofu (silken makes it very creamy)
3 stalks celery, diced	1 tblsp tamari
3 parsnips, diced	1 tblsp whole wheat flour
2 onions or leeks, diced	1 tblsp fresh, or 1 tsp dried, dill weed
½ bunch parsley, chopped	½ tsp dried mustard
½ tsp fennel seed (optional)	
½ cup water	
nutmeg	

1. Sauté vegetables in a small amount of water. Place in baked pie crust.
2. Blend tofu, tamari, flour, dill, mustard, fennel, and water. Pour over vegetables in pie crust. Sprinkle with nutmeg.
3. Bake at 350° for 20 minutes.

More possibilities for vegetable-tofu pie fillings:

corn and broccoli	cauliflower, red pepper, and peas	thinly sliced onions

1. Start with about 6 cups raw vegetables. Preparation is the same.
2. Use this topping or the topping for Spinach, Mushroom, and Tofu Pie.

Note: The vegetables and topping can be placed in lightly oiled ramekins instead of a pie crust. Sprinkle ramekins with whole wheat bread crumbs and/or crunchy wheat and barley cereal, then bake.

Pizza

Crust:

2 cups whole wheat pastry flour	2/3 cup water
2 tsp baking powder	2 tblsp olive oil
2 tblsp soy powder	

1. Combine dry ingredients in a bowl.
2. Add water and oil and stir until dough leaves sides of bowl.
3. Gather together and press into a ball. Knead 10 times, until smooth.
4. Press with fingers to cover bottom and sides of a nonstick 12- by 15-inch pan, making the edge thicker.
5. Preheat oven to 425°.

Topping:

2 or more cups total salsa and/or tomato sauce
grated carrots (or carrot pulp from juicer) and summer squash
thinly sliced onions, bell peppers, and mushrooms
   (a food processor makes short work of it)
broccoli florets
other vegetables, such as sliced tomatoes or celery; chopped green beans,
   edible pod peas, or kale; grated kohlrabi; pressed or finely chopped garlic;
   or bean sprouts
oregano
freshly ground black pepper
8 oz mashed tofu

1. Prepare the vegetables.
2. Spread salsa/tomato sauce over crust.
3. Sprinkle grated vegetables all over, followed by sliced and chopped vegetables, oregano and pepper, and finally tofu.
4. Bake 20-25 minutes, until piping hot.

Pita Pizza

whole wheat pita
salsa or a mix of salsa and tomato sauce
vegetables: grated carrots and summer squash;
    sliced or chopped onions, mushrooms, bell peppers, broccoli; others
oregano
freshly ground black pepper
mashed tofu

Preheat oven to 450°.
1. Place pita rounds (as is or cut around the circumference to create 2 disks) on a nonstick baking sheet. Spread salsa/tomato sauce on pita rounds.
2. Top with grated carrots and squash, then the sliced or chopped vegetables. Sprinkle with oregano and freshly ground black pepper.
3. Spread or sprinkle tofu over all.
4. Bake 8-10 minutes, until piping hot.

Tofu "Steaks"

1 pound (16 oz) tofu, cut into ½-inch slices and pressed (p. 6)
⅔ cup teriyaki sauce (below), miso-fruit sauce (below),
    or other tamari- or miso-based sauces (p. 121, 136, 138)

In a shallow non-stick pan, marinate tofu slices for 30 minutes on each side. Bake or broil, turning when one side is browned.

Teriyaki Sauce

Combine and mix well:

¼ cup tamari	2 cloves garlic, pressed or finely chopped
3 tblsp brown rice vinegar	1 tsp grated fresh, or ½ tsp dried, ginger
2 tblsp rice syrup	¼ tsp dry mustard

Miso-Fruit Sauce

Simmer in a small saucepan:

½ cup miso
1 cup cranberries, raspberries, or blackberries; or ½ cup all-fruit preserves
   (If using cranberries, add 1-2 tblsp rice syrup.)
orange juice to desired thinness

If you make the miso-fruit sauce fairly thick, use it as a topping rather than a marinade:
1. Broil the pressed tofu on both sides until surface is speckled and brown and
   tofu is heated through.
2. Then spread the sauce on one side with a knife, and broil, sauce side up,
   1-2 more minutes.

PONCHO'S WINTER SQUASH OR PUMPKIN PIE

2-3 cups winter squash or pumpkin purée (p. 161)
8 oz tofu, mashed
2 or more cloves garlic, pressed or finely chopped
¼-1 cup chopped onion
2 tblsp tamari
1-1½ cups cooked brown rice (optional)

1. Preheat oven to 350°.
2. Combine all ingredients in a large bowl and mix well. *Or*, to use a food
   processor, drop whole garlic cloves in with the metal blade spinning, and when
   minced, add onion briefly to chop.
3. Add steamed squash or pumpkin, tofu, and tamari, and blend until smooth.
   For a soufflé texture, blend in the rice.
4. Place in a nonstick or lightly oiled pie pan. Bake about 45 minutes.

PUMPKIN-TOFU PATTIES

3 cups well-drained pumpkin or sweet winter squash purée (p. 161)
8-12 oz tofu, pressed (p. 6) and mashed
2 cups cooked grain (optional; it makes the patties firmer)
⅓ cup raisins
freshly ground black pepper

1. Preheat oven to 350°.
2. Blend pumpkin, tofu, and grain by hand or in a processor. Add raisins and pepper.
3. Shape into 2- to 3-inch patties and place on nonstick or lightly oiled baking pan.
4. Bake 20-30 minutes, until browned.

Frozen Tofu "Fish"

1½ cups water
¼ cup tamari
2 tblsp grated fresh, or 2 tsp dried, ginger
1 pound frozen and reconstituted tofu (p. 6) , left in large ⅜-inch slices
   or cut into smaller "fishsticks"
½ cup whole wheat bread flour or mixture of flour and wheat gluten
lemon wedges and ketchup-like sauce (below)

1. Combine water, tamari, and ginger in a saucepan and bring to a boil.
2. Reduce heat to low, add tofu, and simmer 15-20 minutes.
3. Lift out tofu with a slotted spoon or spatula and allow to cool slightly.
4. Preheat oven to 375°.
5. Press each piece of tofu lightly between your hands to expel about ¼ of
   the liquid.
6. Place flour or flour/gluten mixture in a small bowl. Coat each piece of tofu
   and place on nonstick or lightly oiled baking sheet.
7. Bake 10-15 minutes on each side, until nicely browned and crisp.
*Serve with lemon and ketchup-like sauce (below), ketchup (p. 154), chutney
   (p. 155), cranberry condiment (p. 155), or other savory condiment.*

Ketchup-like Sauce
Combine and mix well:

1 small can tomato paste	¼ cup finely chopped onion
2 tsp rice syrup	1 tblsp tamari (optional)
2 tblsp lemon juice	2-4 tblsp Worcestershire sauce (optional)
1-2 cloves garlic, pressed or finely chopped	

BAKED GANMO: TOFU CUTLETS WITH SWEET MISO TOPPING OR NEATBALLS AND SPAGHETTI

12 oz tofu
¼ cup each finely chopped onion, grated carrots, diced mushrooms, and diced celery
2 tblsp total dried sea vegetables: crumbled hijiki, snipped wakame, snipped arame
2 tblsp finely chopped fresh, or 1 tblsp dried, parsley

1. Slice, press, and squeeze the tofu (p. 6-7)
2. Combine tofu and vegetables; mix well. Knead right in the bowl with one hand for 5 minutes, until very smooth.
3. For cutlets, preheat the broiler. Form the mixture into patties. Place on nonstick or lightly oiled baking sheet and broil 6-8 minutes, until nicely browned.
4. Flip, coat with topping (below), and broil 1 minute more. Or, use one of the sauces on p 136.
5. For neatballs, preheat oven to 350°. Form the mixture into small spheres. Place on nonstick or lightly oiled baking sheet.
6. Bake about 10 minutes, until bottoms are brown, then roll them over and bake about 10 more minutes. Place on cooked whole wheat spaghetti and pour salsa/tomato sauce or miso-tahini sauce (p. 136) over all.

Sweet Miso Topping

Combine in a small bowl and mix well:

3 tblsp mellow white miso	1 tsp rice syrup
3 tblsp total mirin and/or brown rice vinegar	1 tsp lemon or lime juice
2 tsp tahini	

TOFU CUBES WITH DIPPING SAUCE

Combine 2 tblsp tamari with any or all of the following:

2 tblsp total lemon or lime juice, mirin, rice vinegar, and/or frozen orange juice concentrate
1 glove garlic, pressed or finely chopped
½ tsp grated fresh, or ¼ tsp dried, ginger

1. Cut tofu into ½-inch cubes and dip into sauce. Or, marinate tofu cubes for several hours.
2. You could also use a miso sauce (below and p. 133), teriyaki sauce (p. 132), lemon-tamari sauce (p. 138), or chutney (p. 155).

Basic Miso Sauce

6 tblsp miso	1 tsp grated lemon rind (optional)
2-4 tblsp rice syrup	½ tsp grated fresh, or ¼ tsp dried, ginger (optional)
2 tblsp total brown rice vinegar, lemon or lime juice, and/or mirin	water

1. Use a light, mellow miso during warmer months, and a dark, strong miso in the winter.
2. Combine ingredients in a small saucepan and simmer over low heat, stirring, for 2-3 minutes. The amount of water to use depends how thick or thin you want the sauce to be.

Miso-Tahini Sauce

To the plain miso sauce, add 4-6 tblsp tahini and 1-2 cloves pressed or finely chopped garlic.

Miso-Mustard Sauce

To the plain miso sauce, add 1 tsp prepared mustard.

OKARA-VEGETABLE BURGERS

Okara, the moist, crunchy by-product of making soymilk (p. 9) is a nutritious, high-fiber food that can be added to soups and grain-and-vegetable dishes and creatively combined with other foods.

For example, make okara burgers by combining okara with finely chopped steamed vegetables, whole wheat flour, and seasonings. Form into burgers, and bake or broil.

Other examples are okara granola (p. 22), okara "feta" (p. 215), and crumbly scrambled okara (p. 83).

TEMPEH

TEMPEH "NOT DOGS"

1 package (8 oz) tempeh	sliced or chopped onions
whole wheat pita	alfalfa or red clover sprouts
sauerkraut	strong mustard
	horseradish (optional)

1. Preheat broiler.
2. Cut tempeh into 16 rectangles for wieners, or 8 longer "not dogs."
3. Place on nonstick or lightly oiled baking sheet and broil on both sides.
4. Use a strainer to drain the sauerkraut, then heat it.
5. Heat pita only until warm and soft. Cut in half to form pockets.
6. Spread mustard and horseradish on pita, and fill with sprouts, tempeh, onions, and, at the last second, very well doubly re-drained sauerkraut (take it out of the pan with a slotted spoon).

Not Dogs go well with non-alcoholic beer.

Alternative: Omit sauerkraut, mustard, and horseradish. Instead, spread miso on one side of the pita and tahini on the other, and add other vegetables such as lettuce and sliced mushrooms and tomatoes.

TEMPEH CACCIATORE OVER RICE

2 packages (16 oz) tempeh	2 cloves garlic, pressed, finely chopped,
1 large onion, diced or thinly sliced	or thinly sliced
into half-rounds	1 tomato, diced
2 bell peppers, diced	oregano; thyme; basil or pesto (p. 91);
1 medium zucchini, quartered lengthwise,	freshly ground black pepper
then diced	2-3 cups total salsa and/or tomato sauce
1½ cups sliced mushrooms	cooked brown rice (p. 2)

1. Preheat oven to 350°.
2. Cut tempeh in half lengthwise, then slice each half crosswise into 3 or 4 wide thin slabs. Place on nonstick or lightly oiled baking sheet and bake until golden, about 5 minutes on each side.
3. Sauté onion, pepper, zucchini, mushrooms, and garlic in a small amount of water.
4. Add diced tomato and seasonings.
5. Heat salsa/tomato sauce.
6. Place rice on plate, top with sautéed vegetables, cover with tempeh slabs, and pour heated salsa/tomato sauce over all.

TEMPEH-NOODLE CASSEROLE

3 cups uncooked pasta
2 cups boiling water
1 cup chopped onion
2 cloves garlic, pressed or finely chopped
2-4 tblsp lemon juice
1 tblsp grated or finely chopped lemon rind
1 cup total chopped canned or fresh tomatoes,
    crushed tomatoes, purée, sauce, and/or salsa
1 cup plain soy yogurt (p. 10)
1 package (8 oz) tempeh
1½ cups stock or mixed vegetable juice
2 tblsp each chopped fresh dill and parsley (or 1 tblsp each, dried)
1 tsp total basil, oregano, and/or savory
1/8 tsp each nutmeg and cinnamon
¼ cup whole wheat bread crumb

1. Cut tempeh into 6 rectangles, then slice each laterally for a total of 12 thin pieces.
2. Preheat oven to 375°.
3. Layer ingredients in the order given in a nonstick or lightly oiled 9-inch square baking pan.
4. Bake uncovered for 1 hour.

TEMPEH "STEAKS"

1 package (8 oz) tempeh	½ cup lemon-tamari sauce (see below)

1. Cut tempeh into 8-12 small pieces, then cut each in half crosswise to make thin rectangles.
2. In a shallow nonstick pan, marinate tempeh slices for 30 minutes on each side. Bake or broil, turning when one side is lightly browned, and cooking only until the other side is also lightly browned.

Lemon-Tamari Sauce

Combine in a 1-cup liquid measuring cup or a small bowl:

¼ cup lemon juice
¼ cup tamari
2 cloves garlic, pressed or finely chopped

Tempeh steaks, mashed potatoes (p. 157), and a fresh salad are a favorite dinner combination.

TEMPEH CHILI

1 cup finely chopped onion
2-3 cloves garlic, pressed or finely chopped
other chopped vegetables, such as bell peppers,
    carrots, celery, corn, mushrooms, and zucchini
1 package (8 oz) tempeh, cubed
1½ tblsp chili powder, or to taste
2 tsp cumin
1 tsp each basil and oregano
½ tsp sage
¼ tsp coriander
¼ tsp cayenne pepper
freshly ground black pepper
6 cups chopped canned or fresh tomatoes, with juice

1. Prepare cumin, basil, oregano, sage, and coriander by grinding in a spice mill or mortar and pestle.
2. Sauté the onions, garlic, and other vegetables in a small amount of water until tender.
3. Add the cubed tempeh and sauté until lightly browned, about 5-10 minutes.
4. Add spices and tomatoes; mix well.
5. Cover and simmer about 30 minutes.

Bean Chili

Replace the sautéed tempeh with 2 cups cooked kidney, pinto, or other beans. You can also add cooked bulgur wheat, or raw bulgur with twice as much water, with the spices and tomatoes.

Even Faster Tempeh Chili

Replace spices and tomatoes with salsa or a mix of salsa and tomato sauce. Simmering time can be shorter.

SWEET AND SOUR TEMPEH

Combine in a small bowl and set aside:

1 tblsp cornstarch (or arrowroot or kuzu: see p. 13)
2 tblsp rice syrup
½ tsp grated fresh, or ¼ tsp dried, ginger
2 tsp tamari
¼ cup brown rice vinegar
½ cup pineapple juice, drained from chunks (see below)

1. Heat a small amount of water in a large skillet.
2. Add and stir-fry about 3 minutes, until crisp-tender :

1 cup bell pepper, cut into 1-inch pieces
1 cup onion, cut into wedges
1 cup carrots, cut into 1/4-inch slices
2 large cloves garlic, pressed or finely chopped
8-oz can sliced water chestnuts, drained (optional)

Add and stir-fry a few minutes:

8-12 oz tempeh, cubed*
1 cup pineapple chunks
½ cup cubed tomatoes, or 2 tblsp tomato sauce or salsa

1. Add sauce. Cook and stir until mixture boils and all ingredients are
   coated with sauce, about 2 minutes.
2. Serve over hot rice.
3. Garnish with chopped scallions or chives if available.

*2 cups cooked soybeans (p. 5) can be substituted for the tempeh.

VEGETABLES

SALADS

RELISHES, AND PICKLES

POTATOES

WINTER SQUASH AND SWEET POTATOES

OTHER VEGETABLE DISHES

SIMPLER VEGETABLE DISHES

Vegetables harvested from your own or a friend's organic garden or a share-farm are the most healthful, satisfying, economical, and energy-efficient. Next freshest would be from a local farmers' market or farm stand. Organic produce is sometimes available at coops, natural foods stores, and supermarkets. It's good for both you and the planet to support organic agriculture.

SALADS

Although many fresh salad vegetables are available all the time, use whatever's in season, so your salad gradually cycles through the year.

torn or coarsely chopped greens: Boston, bibb, romaine, and/or leaf lettuce; chicory, escarole, endive, Chinese cabbage, spinach, mesclun, mustard, celery leaves, parsley, watercress
wild greens: dandelion, lamb's-quarters, sheep sorrel, mint
shredded cabbage: green or red
fresh herbs: basil, dill, summer savory, etc.
sprouts: alfalfa, red clover, radish, mung, others
grated roots: carrots, beets
summer squash: grated zucchini, yellow crookneck, pattypan
cut-up beans: green or wax
peas: shell or cut-up edible pod (snowpeas, sugar peas, snap peas, and sugarsnap peas)
florets: broccoli or cauliflower
edible flowers: calendulas, day lilies, nasturtiums, violas
sliced or chopped: mushrooms, radishes, cucumbers, celery, tomatoes
green, red, or yellow bell peppers: red, yellow, or white onions, scallions (green onions), leeks, shallots, or chives

There are two basic approaches to making a salad:
toss all the prepared vegetables together in a large bowl (then perhaps transfer to a smaller bowl that better fits the amount of tossed salad), or carefully layer the prepared vegetables in a low, wide bowl, and garnish the top with attractive vegetable shapes and colors; for example, green pepper rings and whole tiny tomatoes.

SALAD DRESSING

Choose from the variety of flavorful vinegars one that seems to best accompany your meal. Buy them in bulk or large bottles to refill attractive smaller labeled bottles with inner shaker caps.

The basics:
  apple cider vinegar
  balsamic vinegar
  brown rice vinegar
  red or white wine vinegar
  umeboshi (pickled plum) vinegar

Among the more unusual vinegars are mint vinegar and champagne vinegar. Some bottled vinegars contain herb sprigs, or you can add them yourself.

Give vinegar a chance as salad dressing. Before long, you may not want to pour anything heavier on those delicate, flavorful vegetables.

But here are some alternatives. These can also be served over cooked grain and vegetable dishes.

Oilless Vinaigrette

½ cup red wine vinegar
¼ cup water
1-2 cloves garlic,
   pressed or finely chopped
¼ cup chopped onion, or any member of the onion family

½ tsp dried mustard
1 tblsp chopped fresh basil,
   or ½ tsp dried basil
freshly grated black pepper

Combine in a small pitcher and mix well, or combine in a jar and shake well.

Lemon-Sesame Dressing

1-2 cloves garlic,
   pressed or finely chopped*
¼ cup chopped onions or scallions
¼ cup finely chopped bell pepper

½ cup lemon or lime juice
2 tblsp tamari
2 tblsp tahini
¼ tsp celery seeds

Blend all.

If using a food processor, drop in whole garlic cloves with metal blade spinning to mince, add onion and bell pepper to chop, then add remaining ingredients.

Gazpacho Dressing

6 ounces tomato juice
slice of garlic
1-2 tblsp total vinegar and/or lemon juice
1-inch by 3-inch strip of bell pepper
slice of onion or a small scallion
2-inch section of cucumber
sprig of parsley
small amount of fresh or dried green herbs,
   such as basil, dill, marjoram, tarragon
freshly ground black pepper

Purée in a blender or processor. Chill.

Tahini-Tamari or Tahini-Miso Dressing

4 tblsp tahini
4 tblsp tamari or 2 tblsp miso
2 tblsp lemon, lime, or orange juice;
    or balsamic, brown rice, or red wine vinegar
1 tblsp mirin (optional)
water to desired consistency
finely chopped onions or green onions (optional)
pressed or finely chopped garlic (optional)

1. Blend tahini, tamari or miso, juice or vinegar, and mirin.
2. Add water. Stir in onions and/or garlic.

Dilled Soygurt Dressing

1 cup plain soy yogurt (p. 10)
2 tblsp vinegar
½ cup chopped onion

½ tsp dill seeds
½ tsp dry mustard
1 clove garlic, pressed or finely chopped

Mix well or purée in a blender or processor.

Tofu "Mayonnaise"

6 oz tofu
    cayenne
2 tblsp lemon juice or brown rice vinegar

freshly ground black pepper or pinch of

¼ tsp dry, or ½ tsp prepared, mustard
    (optional)

1. Purée in a blender or processor until totally smooth, adding water to desired consistency.
2. Curry powder, pressed or finely chopped garlic, and/or herbs are other possible additions.

RELISHES AND PICKLES

EGGPLANT RELISH

4-5 cups chunked peeled eggplant (1 large)
1 cup finely chopped onions
1 cup finely chopped bell peppers

2 or more garlic cloves, pressed or finely chopped
¼ cup or more lemon juice or brown rice vinegar
freshly ground black pepper

1. Steam eggplant until very soft. Press out liquid, and chop.
2. Combine with remaining ingredients and mix well. Use as a side dish, dip, or on sandwiches (see p. 70).

SPICY EGGPLANT RELISH

4-5 cups chunked peeled eggplant (1 large)
1 cup chopped onions
2 or more garlic cloves,
    pressed or finely chopped
1 tsp grated fresh, or ¼ tsp dried, ginger
1 tsp ground coriander seed
½ tsp ground cumin seed

¼ tsp turmeric
½ tsp hot sauce
1 cup diced tomatoes
2 tblsp finely chopped fresh parsley,
    or 2 tsp finely chopped fresh coriander leaf
¼ cup soy yogurt (optional)

1. Prepare eggplant as above. Sauté onions, garlic, and spices in a small amount of water. Add tomato and cook a few more minutes.
2. Place in serving bowl and stir in parsley or coriander and soy yogurt.
3. Serve warm or cold.

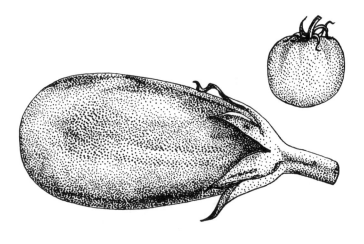

MARINATED BROCCOLI

florets from 1 head broccoli	freshly ground black pepper
¼ cup lemon juice	1 clove garlic, pressed or minced

1. Steam florets until bright green and crisp-tender. Place in a bowl.
2. Combine dressing ingredients and pour over hot broccoli. Chill.

MARINATED ZUCCHINI AND MUSHROOMS

Vegetables	*Dressing*
4 cups thinly sliced zucchini	½ cup red or white wine vinegar,
2 cups sliced mushroom	or other vinegar
1 cup diced tomato	1-2 cloves garlic,
2 tblsp finely chopped	pressed or finely chopped
onion or scallion	1 tsp dried marjoram
	1 tblsp chopped fresh, or
	1 tsp dried, mint leaves
	freshly ground black pepper

1. Steam the zucchini or sauté it in a small amount of water until tender.
2. Place in a bowl and let cool. Toss with the other vegetables.
3. Combine dressing ingredients, pour over vegetables, and toss. Chill.

SWEET AND SOUR VEGETABLE SALAD

Vegetables

2 cups thinly sliced zucchini or cucumber
½ cup each chopped bell pepper and celery
¼ cup chopped onion
other vegetables, such as chopped tomatoes or sliced mushrooms (optional)

If you add other vegetables, increase the amount of dressing.

Dressing

½ cup wine or cider vinegar
2 tblsp rice syrup
freshly ground black pepper
snipped fresh dill (optional)

Pour dressing over prepared vegetables. Chill.

SWEET AND SOUR BEAN SPROUTS

½ cup water
2 cups mung bean sprouts
1 tblsp rice syrup

¼ cup wine vinegar or brown rice vinegar
freshly ground black pepper

1. Heat water. Add sprouts and rice syrup, and cook 1 minute while stirring.
2. Drain and cool.
3. Toss with vinegar and pepper. Marinate in refrigerator.

COOKED SWEET AND SOUR VEGETABLES

Vegetables

4 cups thinly sliced summer squash - crookneck, pattypan, zucchini
½ cup each slivered bell pepper, thinly sliced carrots, and thinly sliced onion
½ cup each of several other vegetables,
    such as beans, broccoli, cabbage, cauliflower, celery, kale, mushrooms
2 tblsp sea vegetables (optional)

Dressing

2 tblsp wine vinegar
2 tblsp apple cider vinegar
1-2 cloves garlic, pressed or finely chopped
freshly ground black pepper
herbs to taste, such as basil, dill, dry mustard or mustard seed,
    marjoram, oregano, thyme
1 tblsp rice syrup

1. Steam vegetables over boiling water until crisp-tender. Place in a bowl.
2. Combine vinegar and herbs, pour over cooked vegetables, and toss.
    Drain off some liquid into a very small pot.
3. Stir in rice syrup to dissolve, then return mixture to bowl. Toss again.

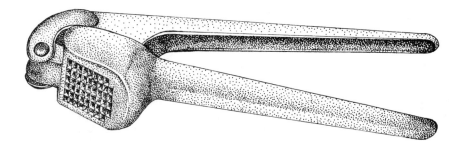

Sylvia's Basic ColeSlaw

Vegetables

Use the thin slicing or shredding disc of a food processor. If using the slicing disc,
cut the carrots and peppers lengthwise first.
Combine in a large bowl:

4 cups thinly sliced or shredded green cabbage
1 cup thinly sliced or shredded carrots
1 cup thinly sliced or shredded green,
    yellow and/or red bell peppers

Dressing

Combine, pour over vegetables,
    and toss well.

scant half cup apple cider vinegar
generous ¼ cup water
1 clove garlic, pressed or
    finely chopped
dash olive oil

Pseudo-sauerkraut

Use cabbage, vinegar, and water only,
    and let marinate in the refrigerator.

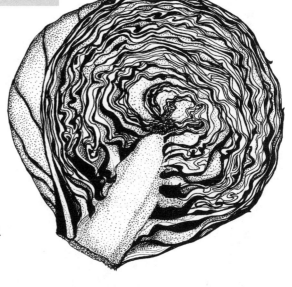

ColeSlaw

Vegetables

Combine in a large bowl:

4 cups shredded cabbage
1 cup diced celery
1 cup shredded or grated carrot
1 cup total finely chopped
    green, yellow, or red peppers
½ cup chopped parsley
½ cup chopped onions,
    scallions, or chives
½ cup chopped cucumber

Dressing

Blend, pour over vegetables, and toss well:

¼ cup vinegar
2 tblsp lemon juice
2 tblsp rice syrup
1-2 cloves garlic, pressed
    or finely chopped
½ tsp celery seed
½ tsp curry powder (optional)
freshly ground black pepper

Horseradish

Cut fresh horseradish root into small cubes. Grate in a food processor using the metal blade and pulse motion. The fumes are powerful, so remove the lid slowly, with your face averted. Transfer to a small container and add as much white vinegar as the horseradish will absorb.

Tightly covered in the refrigerator, it will keep about two weeks. For long-term storage, transfer to hot, sterilized half-pint (1-cup) canning jars, wipe rims with a clean cloth, cap with sterilized lids and rings, and process in a boiling water bath for 20 minutes. (After jars have sealed, remove rings to store.)

Corn Relish

8-10 ears of corn	1½ cups cider vinegar
1 cup diced green peppers	¼ cup rice syrup
1 cup diced red peppers	1 tsp celery seed
1 cup finely chopped celery	1½ tsp total dry mustard and/or
½ cup minced onion	crushed mustard seed

1. Steam corn 5 minutes, cool, and cut off kernels. In a large pot, combine vegetables, vinegar, rice syrup, and celery seed. Boil 5 minutes.
2. Mix the mustard with a small amount of liquid and return to the pot. Add corn and cook 5 minutes, stirring occasionally. This goes nicely with mochi (p. 99).

Pickles

Bring to a boil 2 cups water for every 1 cup vinegar (use white or apple cider vinegar).

Put in hot, sterilized pint or quart mason jars:

1 tsp canning salt per quart	1 clove garlic, whole, sliced, or coarsely chopped
1 tsp mustard seed	1 hot pepper or some scraped horseradish
½ dill seed head and some dill weed	(optional)

1. Wash gherkin-size cucumbers. Leave a bit of stem on. Pack into jars.
2. Fill with boiling liquid, leaving ¼-inch head space. Wipe rims with a clean cloth, and cap with sterilized lids and rings.
3. For long-term storage, process in a boiling water bath for 15 minutes. (After jars have sealed, remove rings to store.) Keep in a dark, dry, cool place.

Note: You can do the same with slices or spears of larger cucumbers, small green tomatoes, tiny onions, cauliflowerets, and sliced onions, carrots, celery, and bell peppers. Try a combination in the same jar. Pack whole string beans (green, yellow, purple) vertically into pint jars.

Marinated Kirby Cukes

1. Kirby cucumbers are small and unwaxed. Thinly slice the cucumbers.
2. Prepare a marinade of two parts apple cider vinegar to one part water, with an optional dash of olive oil.
3. Cover the cucumber slices with the marinade and store in the refrigerator.
4. Use as pickles. They're salt-free and they'll keep indefinitely.

Pickled Beets

1 quart small beets, or sliced or diced larger beets
½ cup apple cider vinegar
2-4 tblsp rice syrup
1 red onion, thinly sliced
½ tsp kelp powder, optional
3 tsp fresh tarragon, or 1 tsp dried tarragon

1. Steam beets until tender.
2. Heat vinegar, rice syrup, onion, kelp, and tarragon to the boiling point. Cool.
3. Pour over the beets and mix well. Chill.

Spicy Chickpeas with Tomato Sauce

1 tblsp each coriander and cumin seeds
½ tsp turmeric
1 tsp each oregano and paprika
small amounts of cinnamon, cloves, crushed cardamom, white pepper
½ cup sliced onions
3 cups cooked (or canned) chickpeas (p. 5), drained
1 cup total salsa and/or tomato sauce
2 tsp grated fresh, or 1 tsp dried, ginger
2 tblsp chopped parsley

1. Crush the seeds in a mortar and pestle or grind them coarsely with a spice mill
2. Heat a small amount of water, and sauté spices for 5 minutes.
   Add more water if needed.
3. Add onions and sauté until soft.
4. Add the chickpeas, salsa/tomato sauce, and ginger, and simmer 5-7 minutes.
5. Garnish with parsley.

KETCHUP

about 3 cups

2 quarts peeled, cored, chopped red-ripe tomatoes (about 12 large)
½ cup chopped onion
¼ cup chopped sweet red peppers
¼ cup rice syrup
whole spices: ¾ tsp celery seed, ½ tsp mustard seed, ½ tsp whole allspice,
   and 1 stick cinnamon, tied in a cheesecloth bag
½ cup vinegar
½ tsp paprika

1. To quickly peel tomatoes, drop briefly into boiling water and retrieve.
   The skins will slip off.
2. Cook tomatoes, onions, and pepper until soft. Then cook rapidly until thick,
   about 1 hour. Volume will be reduced by half.
3. Stir in rice syrup. Place bag of spices in pan.
4. Cook gently about 25 minutes, stirring frequently.
5. Add vinegar and paprika.
6. Cook until thick, stirring frequently to prevent sticking.

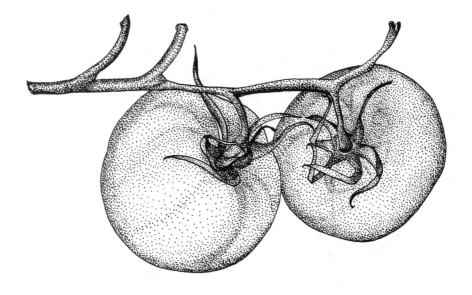

INDIAN CHUTNEY

4 cups chopped apples
¼ cup lemon or lime juice
¾ cup apple juice
¼ cup apple cider vinegar
½ cup currants or raisins

1 cup chopped dates
2-4 tblsp rice syrup
1 tsp coriander seeds, ground*
1-2 tblsp dark miso

1. Combine all ingredients except the miso in a saucepan.
2. Bring to a boil, cover, and cook until apples are tender, about 10 minutes.
3. Remove from heat and stir in miso until dissolved.

*You can leave some whole if you won't be eating the chutney until the next day.

SWEET INDIAN CHUTNEY

Omit the vinegar and reduce the rice syrup.

CRANBERRY CONDIMENT

1. Simply cook fresh or frozen berries with a small amount of water for about 10 minutes, until they are easily mashed.
2. Mash them and stir in some rice syrup and orange or other fruit juice.
3. You can stop now or, for a thicker sauce, continue simmering, partly covered, to desired thickness, stirring occasionally.*

SPICY SWEET AND SOUR CRANBERRY CONDIMENT *

4 cups cranberries, cooked and mashed
1 tsp each cinnamon, cloves, and allspice
¼ cup rice syrup
¼ cup orange or apple juice concentrate
¾ cup cider vinegar
freshly ground black pepper

1. Add remaining ingredients to the cooked, mashed cranberries.
2. With the pan partly covered, boil down to desired consistency, stirring occasionally.

CRANBERRY CONDIMENT WITH RAISINS *

3 cups cranberries	¼-½ cup rice syrup
1 cup raisins or currants	1½ cups apple juice or cider
2 tblsp grated fresh ginger	

1. Combine in a pot. Bring to a simmer.
2. Reduce heat and cook gently, stirring frequently, until the cranberries soften, about 10 minutes.

These cranberry condiments can be stored in the refrigerator or freezer. Or, follow the canning instructions for pumpkin conserve on page 204.

POTATOES

BAKED POTATOES

1. Preheat oven to 400°.
2. Peel potatoes, rinse, and stab with a fork or small knife in several places.
3. Place directly on oven racks and bake until fork-tender, ½-1 hour, depending on the size of the potatoes.
4. Break open, and eat plain or top with any combination of

freshly ground black pepper	chopped chives or scallions
hot sauce	tamari
fresh or dried parsley	plain soy yogurt (p. 10)

Once they're baked, the sooner they're eaten, the better they taste.

You don't want to keep them in the oven once they're ready. We keep them warm out of the oven by wrapping them in a dishtowel and then a blanket or sleeping bag! Enough of these, with a big, fresh salad, is dinner.

Bake extras to make oven-roasted potatoes (p. 158) or baked vegetable chips (p. 169).

MASHED POTATOES

You can water-sauté leftover mashed potatoes or use them in other recipes
  (p. 112, 158), so you may as well cook more than you can eat.
1. Peel (or for new potatoes, just scrub) and cut up the potatoes. The smaller the pieces, the shorter the cooking time (and the less energy used).
2. Place in a pot with just ½-1 inch of water, cover, bring to a boil, then reduce heat and simmer until potatoes are so soft they fall apart when touched with a fork. Add more water if needed to prevent sticking.
3. Remove pot from burner and place on a potholder or hotplate. Mash thoroughly with a potato masher. (Whipping breaks down the complex-carbohydrate structure and makes the potatoes gooey.)
4. Add more hot water while mashing if you like it thinner.
5. Serve with freshly ground black pepper, hot sauce, fresh or dried parsley, chopped chives or scallions, plain soy yogurt (p. 10), and/or tamari.

GARLIC MASHED POTATOES

1. Peel up to 15 cloves of garlic for each pound of raw potatoes.
2. Steam the garlic about 20 minutes, until very tender but not brown. Or, steam before peeling, then cool slightly and slip off the peels.
3. Add to steamed potatoes before mashing.

LEEK MASHED POTATOES

1. Finely dice up to 3 cups of leeks for each pound of raw potatoes. (First cut off root ends, split leeks lengthwise almost through to end, rinse between leaves, then dice.)
2. Steam in a small amount of water until wilted, cover, and cook on a low heat about 10 minutes.
3. Add to steamed potatoes before mashing.

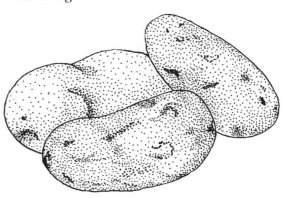

Baked Mashed Potato Quiche

4-6 cups just-cooked or leftover mashed potatoes
¼ cup finely chopped onion
2 or more cloves garlic, pressed or finely chopped
4-6 oz mashed fresh tofu or whipped silken soft tofu
2 tblsp chopped fresh, or 2 tsp dried, parsley
¼ tsp paprika or ⅛ tsp cayenne
freshly ground black pepper

1. Preheat oven to 400°.
2. Combine all ingredients and spread evenly in that indispensable 12- by 15-inch nonstick baking pan.
3. Other herb blends of your choice will give the quiche its special flavor.
4. Bake until crisp and crusty, about 45 minutes. Good with hot sauce, tamari, or plain soy yogurt (p. 10).

Steamed Potatoes

1. Peel (or for new potatoes, just scrub) and cut up the potatoes to desired size. (Leave tiny potatoes whole.)
2. Steam over boiling water about 15 minutes, until tender.
3. Serve with freshly ground black pepper, hot sauce, chopped chives, fresh or dried parsley or dill, plain soy yogurt (p. 10), and/or tamari.

Oven-Roasted Potatoes

4 large leftover baked potatoes or equivalent   1 tsp dried parsley
1 cup chopped onions   1 tsp paprika
2 tblsp tamari

1. Preheat oven to 400°.
2. Cut potatoes into 1/4-inch slices and arrange on a nonstick baking pan.
3. Top with the onions, tamari, parsley, and paprika.
4. Cover and bake 20-30 minutes, until piping hot and beginning to crisp.

Note: You can start with steamed potatoes that have been chilled.
Or, you can start with raw potatoes. Bake 50-60 minutes.

KING TOYETTES

1. Heat a dry cast-iron skillet or griddle to medium-high.
2. Thinly slice (about ¼ inch) enormous potatoes.
3. Dry-fry slices on one side until they blister, flip and do the same.
4. Keep stovetop fan on to exhaust the cooking smoke.

Good with salsa, ketchup-like sauce (p. 122), or ketchup (p. 139).

PAUL'S HASH-BROWN POTATOES

chopped green onions	freshly ground black pepper
diced or sliced potatoes	cayenne

1. In a skillet, "steam-fry" the onions (sauté them in a small amount of hot water), then add potatoes, pepper, and cayenne.
2. Cover, cook 15-20 minutes over medium-low heat, turn over and keep cooking until potatoes are all soft and browned.
3. Serve with ketchup (p. 154) or ketchup-like sauce (p. 134).

HUSH KUSKIS (POTATO NOODLES)

3/4 cup finely grated raw potatoes	¼ cup wheat gluten
½ cup whole wheat bread flour	¼ cup cold water

1. Bring 4 quarts of water to a boil.
2. Mix well. Form into 1/4-inch noodles, or into any shapes. Drop one at a time into the boiling water.
3. Cook 15 minutes, stirring frequently, then drain.
4. Bake at 400° about 15 minutes, turning once.

For a "fish 'n' chips" dinner, have Hush Kuskis and Frozen Tofu "Fish" (p. 134) with cranberry condiment (p. 155) or ketchup-like sauce (p. 134) and a fresh green salad.

POTATO PANCAKES

3 large potatoes, or equivalent, peeled	1 stalk celery
1 large onion or equivalent	1 or more carrots
1-2 cloves garlic, finely chopped	1 small zucchini (optional)

1 sprig parsley, finely chopped, or 1 tsp dried parsley
¼ cup total whole wheat flour, wheat gluten, bread crumbs, soy powder, and/or bran
freshly ground black pepper
4 ounces tofu, mashed (optional; see below)

1. Heat a nonstick baking pan as you preheat the oven to 400°.
2. Grate the potatoes, onion, celery, carrot, and zucchini by hand, or use the shredding disc of a food processor followed by the metal blade. Drain off liquid.
3. Mash together with remaining ingredients, or using the processor's metal blade, chop the parsley and garlic, add everything else, and pulse to purée to desired smoothness. (If you're blending the ingredients by hand, the tofu will help keep the pancakes cohesive.) You can also purée the mixture in several batches in a blender.
4. Drop by tablespoons onto hot pan. Bake about 20 minutes on each side. Serve with applesauce (p. 207), other fruit sauce, and/or soy yogurt (p. 10).

POTATO KUGEL

1. Grate or shred the vegetables by hand or with a food processor.
2. Spread evenly in one or two nonstick or lightly oiled baking pans.
3. Bake at 350° for about 45 minutes, until edges are dry and kugel is nicely browned.

LATKES

4 medium to large potatoes, peeled and chopped
about half as many chopped carrots as potatoes
about half as much chopped celery as carrots
about half as much chopped pineapple as celery
dash to ¼ tsp nutmeg
4-8 ounces tofu, mashed (optional)

1. Place potatoes, carrots, and celery in a pot with ½-1 inch of water, cover, bring to a boil, then reduce heat and simmer. Add water if needed to prevent sticking.
2. While the vegetables cook, heat a nonstick or lightly oiled baking pan as you preheat the oven to 400°.
3. When vegetables are soft, remove from heat and mash. Add pineapple and nutmeg (and tofu). Drop by tablespoons or larger spoonfuls onto hot pan. Flatten larger latkes somewhat. Bake about 20 minutes on each side.
4. Or, for kugel, spread the mixture in nonstick or lightly oiled baking pans and bake at 350° for about 45 minutes, until edges are dry and kugel is nicely browned.
5. Serve with applesauce (p. 207) or baked apples (p. 205) and soy yogurt.

WI TER SQUASH A D SWEET POTATOES

WINTER SQUASH OR PUMPKIN PURÉE

Each pound of raw squash or pumpkin yields about 1 cup of purée, although the more watery, the less purée.

STEAMED WINTER SQUASH OR PUMPKIN

Rinse a squash or pumpkin. Halve it with a heavy knife (and some persuasion from a rubber mallet, if needed) and remove strings and seeds with a large spoon. (The seeds can be removed from the strings and baked - see p. 212.) Cleave into sections and steam, rind side down, in a small amount of water (about ½ inch) in a large covered pot until completely soft, 20-40 minutes. Remove from heat and, when cool, scoop squash or pumpkin from rind. You may be surprised to find that some cooked squash rind makes a delicious snack for the cook! Mash the pulp with a potato masher or purée in a food processor. It freezes well, so you can cook a squash or pumpkin as soon as you see a soft spot, then have the purée conveniently ready to defrost when you need it. Refrigerate the steaming liquid for sautéing and soup stock.

Some squash and pumpkins are more watery than others. For cooking, the less watery the steamed pulp, the better. So drain off the excess, using a masher " and/or strainer to help extract water. Keep this precious liquid, too, for sautéing and soup stock.

BAKED WINTER SQUASH OR PUMPKIN

Squash and pumpkins can also be baked, but it uses more energy and takes longer. Place halves cut-side down on a nonstick baking pan, pour some water on the pan, and bake at 350° about an hour. Turn squash over, pour some orange or pineapple juice into the cavities (baking yields drier pulp than steaming), and bake another 10-30 minutes, until fork tender. Cool, scoop from rind, and mash or purée as above.

STEAMED OR BAKED WINTER SQUASH

Some winter squash are so sweet, they can be steamed or baked (above) and eaten as is, right off the rind, with a grain dish and a salad. Or, put some rice syrup, raisins, ginger, and/or cinnamon in the cavities during or after cooking.

Mashed Sweet Potatoes or Winter Squash

Peel, chunk, and steam sweet potatoes until soft, or cook an acorn, buttercup, butternut, delicata, small Hokkaido or Hubbard, or other sweet winter squash (see previous page). Add a small amount orange juice, pineapple juice, or other fruit juice for extra sweetness as you mash the squash or sweet potatoes or purée them in a processor.

Fruited Winter Squash

2-3 cups diced steamed winter squash (see below)	2 tblsp rice syrup
1 cup cranberries	juice of one lime
2 clementines, tangerines, or mandarin oranges, peeled	dash of cinnamon
1-2 cups chopped peeled apples and/or small pineapple chunks	small amount finely minced fresh mint (optional, of course)

Halve an acorn, buttercup, butternut, delicata, small Hokkaido or Hubbard, or other sweet winter squash and remove the seeds. Cleave into sections and steam over boiling water until just on the verge of tenderness. (You don't want it to get mushy when mixed with the other ingredients.) Remove from pot, cool, scrape free from rind, and dice.

While squash steams, chop the cranberries in a food processor and prepare the other fruit. (Cut clementine segments into small pieces with a sharp knife or scissors.) Combine fruit in a bowl with the rice syrup, lime juice, cinnamon, and mint. Carefully fold in the squash. Let sit a few hours before serving, or refrigerate overnight, then reheat.

Apple-Stuffed Winter Squash

1 large or 2 smaller sweet winter squash, such as acorn, butternut, or delicata, halved or sliced (see below)	raisins, dried cranberries, or ground fresh cranberries
chopped apples or applesauce	small amounts of rice syrup and lemon or orange juice
small pineapple chunks (optional)	

1. Preheat oven to 400°.
2. Combine stuffing ingredients. Spoon into squash halves.
3. Place in ½ inch water in a baking dish. Cover and bake 30 minutes; remove cover and bake until tender, about 30 more minutes.
4. Or, steam sliced squash until tender, about 20 minutes. Heat the stuffing ingredients, and spoon over steamed squash.

Spaghetti Squash

Steam or bake a spaghetti squash (p. 161). Scoop out strands with a fork and serve like pasta with tomato sauce and/or salsa (see p. 90), or tossed with a mix of vegetables and seasonings, such as:

2 cups chopped tomatoes
1 cup diced cucumbers
½ cup diced red onions
1 or more cloves garlic, pressed or finely chopped
other vegetables, such as sliced celery and mushrooms;
   diced bell pepper and carrots; broccoli florets
½ cup chopped fresh, or 2 tblsp dried, parsley
¼ cup chopped fresh, or 1 tblsp dried, basil
2-4 tblsp lemon juice
freshly ground black pepper

Traditional Sweet Potatoes and Apples

4-5 cups sliced sweet potatoes
3 cups peeled, cored, and sliced apples
cranberries (optional, good at holiday time)
¼ cup apple juice, cider, or orange juice

1. Preheat oven to 350°.
2. In a 1½-quart baking dish or casserole, arrange layers of sweet potatoes and apples, sprinkling cranberries here and there. Pour the juice over.
3. Cover and bake 1 hour, then uncover and bake 15 more minutes.

Note: To save energy, steam the sweet potatoes, apples, and cranberries until soft, then serve immediately; or steam until crisp-tender, then assemble as a casserole and bake until piping hot. Or, purée cooked sweet potatoes and apples with orange juice, lemon juice, ground ginger, and cinnamon.

Stovetop Sweet Sweet Potatoes

cubed sweet potatoes	cubed apples
cubed carrots	1 can of unsweetened pineapple chunks, drained

1. Use some of the juice from the pineapple to steam the cubed sweet potatoes and carrots until they just begin to soften.
2. Add cubed apples.
3. When all is tender, stir in pineapple and heat through.

SWEET POTATO PIE

4 cups peeled, cubed, and steamed sweet potatoes
1 cup chopped fresh or canned pineapple
½ cup chopped apples
½ cup cooked grits or couscous

½ tsp each grated ginger and nutmeg
4 oz tofu
chopped roasted chestnuts (p. 213),
    optional

1. Preheat oven to 350°.
2. Purée everything except the chestnuts in a food processor, or mash and mix it all together. Stir in the chestnuts.
3. Place mixture in a nonstick or lightly oiled pie pan.
4. Bake until piping hot, about 20-30 minutes.

BAKED SWEET POTATOES

sweet potatoes
fruit-only jam
orange juice or other fruit juice
grated lemon rind

sliced or chopped apples
raisins
crushed unsweetened pineapple
cinnamon

1. Preheat oven to 400°.
3. Peel the sweet potatoes, or just scrub and remove unsightly spots. Cut lengthwise into halves or quarters, slice, or cut into chunks or cubes. Place on baking dish. Spread, pour, and sprinkle on any or all of the remaining ingredients. Cover and bake until tender, about 30 minutes.

TSIMMES

cubed sweet potatoes*
sliced carrots
pineapple juice or orange juice
diced apples

cut-up pitted prunes
pineapple chunks or tidbits
mandarin orange sections

In a saucepan, steam sweet potatoes and carrots in juice until just soft. Add remaining ingredients and heat through. (To make tidbits, which are hard to find in large cans, stack up the contents of a can of pineapple rings and slice across and through the whole stack in several places.)

Serve any sweet potato dish with or over a light grain such as millet, couscous, or quinoa. Add a salad and you have a meal.

*It's not traditional, but sweet winter squash can be used instead of sweet potatoes. Raw winter squash is hard to peel. It's easier to halve and seed the squash, cut it into quarters, sixths, or eighths, steam it until just beginning to soften, let it cool, and then peel and cube it.

OTHER VEGETABLE DISHES

CAULIFLOWER WITH ONIONS, TOMATOES, AND TAHINI

2 large Spanish or Vidalia onions, finely sliced
2 tblsp sea vegetables (optional)
1 tblsp rice syrup
florets from one head cauliflower
½ cup total chopped tomatoes, tomato juice, and/or tomato sauce
2 tblsp tahini

1. Sauté the onions (and sea vegetables) in a small amount of water until onions are tender and lightly browned.
2. Add rice syrup and cook 2 more minutes.
3. Add florets and tomato.
4. Cover and cook over medium heat until the cauliflower is crisp-tender.
5. Stir in the tahini and serve.

CURRIED CAULIFLOWER

1 head cauliflower
¼ tsp mustard seeds
2-3 cloves garlic, pressed or finely chopped
1 cup finely chopped onions
1 cup total diced tomato, tomato sauce, and/or salsa
1 cup soy yogurt (p. 10) or about 1/4 cup water
1 tsp grated fresh, or ¼ tsp dried, ginger
½ tsp ground cumin (or crushed seeds)
½ tsp ground coriander (or crushed seeds)
½ tsp turmeric

1. Cut the cauliflower into small florets and thinly slice the stems. Steam about 6 minutes, until crisp-tender.
2. Heat a small amount of water in a skillet. Add the mustard seeds and stir until they soften. Add the garlic and onions and cook until soft.
3. Add tomato, soy yogurt or water, and spices. Heat to boiling, stir in cauliflower, reduce heat to low, cover, and cook 10 minutes.
4. This is excellent with a fresh salad and a side dish of wheat berries (p. 4) and currants or raisins.

ORIGINAL SUCCOTASH

The basic vegetables of North America weren't imported from Europe. Traditional Native American gardens centered around the "Three Sisters of Life": corn, beans, and squash.

Remove kernels from corn, shell fresh lima or other shell beans, and cut summer squash into small pieces. Place in a pot with a small amount of water. Cover and steam over medium heat, stirring occasionally, until tender, less than 10 minutes.

LATE-SUMMER SUCCOTASH

1 cup finely chopped onion
1½ cups corn kernels, fresh (cut from about 3 ears) or frozen
3 cups zucchini, quartered lengthwise and cut crosswise into ½-inch slices
3 cups halved or quartered cherry tomatoes
  or larger tomatoes cut into small sections
1 tsp each basil and oregano
freshly ground black pepper

1. Sauté the onion in a large nonstick skillet in a small amount of water until soft. Add the remaining ingredients and toss lightly.
2. Cover and cook over medium-low heat for 15 minutes, stirring gently a few times. This is another good use for a giant zucchini overlooked for too long in the garden.

MID-WINTER SUCCOTASH

2 cups cooked dried lima beans (p. 5)
½ cup sliced onions
2 cloves garlic, pressed or finely chopped
2 cups corn kernels (frozen during corn's late-summer high season)
2 cups peeled, cubed winter squash, steamed just until tender
  (Peeling is easier if you steam unpeeled squash sections first,
  just until the verge of tenderness, then cool, scrape from rind, and cube.)

1. Sauté onions and garlic in a small amount of water until limp.
2. Add limas, corn, and squash and heat through.

This is good as is, or with miso sauce (p. 136) or baked or steamed chestnuts (p. 213).
You could also peel the cooked chestnuts, cut or break them into several pieces, and mix them in as you finish heating the succotash.

Baked Tomatoes and/or Zucchini

tomatoes, cut in half (and/or zucchini, sliced and steamed; see below)
garlic, pressed or finely chopped, or thinly sliced and/or minced onion
finely chopped fresh parsley, or dried parsley
dried rosemary and basil
freshly ground black pepper
whole wheat bread crumbs

1. Preheat oven to 400°.

Simplest: Arrange the tomatoes, cup side up, in a baking dish and bake about 30 minutes until soft and sizzling.

Also quick and easy: Sprinkle tomatoes with garlic and/or onion, parsley, rosemary, and pepper before baking. Chopped bell pepper can also be used.

A little more involved: Combine garlic and/or onion, bread crumbs, herbs, and pepper. (You can chop the garlic or onion in a food processor, then continue to process with cubed bread slices, herbs, and pepper.) Scatter the mixture over tomatoes and/or sliced, steamed zucchini, then bake. Or water-sauté the garlic or onions first, prepare the bread crumb mixture, and alternate in layers with the tomatoes or zucchini in a smaller, deeper baking dish. Cover and bake about 15 minutes.

To turn it into a dinner entrée: Stir mashed pressed or firm tofu into the bread crumb mixture.

Stuffed tomatoes: Preheat oven to 350°. Cut tops off whole tomatoes and remove the pulp. Chop the pulp, and add it to the bread crumb mixture. Fill the tomatoes and place in a nonstick baking dish just large enough to hold them. (If there's extra stuffing, place it in the bottom of the dish and place the tomatoes on top.) Bake 15 minutes. You can use any stuffing, such as on p. 101, 106, 107, and 115.

Stovetop Summer Squash and Tomatoes

4 medium zucchini, yellow crookneck, or pattypan squash, thickly sliced or chunked	½ cup chopped bell pepper
	1 tsp chopped fresh, or ½ tsp dried, basil
4 cups chopped tomatoes	1 tsp chopped fresh, or ½ tsp dried, oregano
1 cup chopped onions	2 tblsp chopped fresh, or 1 tblsp dried, parsley
2 cloves garlic, pressed or finely chopped	2 tsp lemon juice

1. Steam squash until tender.
2. Meanwhile, combine remaining ingredients in a skillet and cook until thick.
3. Add squash, cover, and simmer several minutes.
4. Serve with fresh wholegrain bread or a cooked whole grain, and a salad.

BEETS, CORN, AND TOMATOES—AN AUGUST MÉLANGE

1-2 cups quartered, sliced, and steamed beets (and chopped stems)
1-2 cups corn kernels, sliced from ears and steamed
2 cups chunked tomatoes
2 tblsp total chopped fresh herbs of your choice:
    basil, savory, tarragon, marjoram, rosemary
freshly ground black pepper
¼ cup red wine vinegar blended with 1 tsp prepared mustard

1. Let beets and corn cool.
2. Combine with tomatoes, herbs, and pepper, then toss with vinegar mixture.

RED CABBAGE AND APPLES

4 cups shredded red cabbage   1-2 tblsp rice syrup
1½ cups cored, sliced apples   ½ tsp cinnamon
½ cup apple cider vinegar freshly ground black pepper
    raisins (optional)

1. Combine all ingredients in a saucepan.
2. Cover tightly and cook over medium heat for 10 minutes,
    until cabbage is just tender.
3. Uncover and stir another 1-2 minutes.

CREAMED ONIONS

onions - leave tiny ones whole; cut larger ones into quarters or eighths
soy powder
herbs and seasonings (see below)

1. Steam onions over simmering water until tender.
2. In a separate pan, mix equal parts of soy powder
    and water, stirring until smooth. (Or, steam the
    onions first and use the steaming-water.)
3. Add chopped fresh and/or dried herbs, such
    as basil, parsley, rosemary, savory, tarragon,
    and thyme. Or, use a pinch each of dry
    mustard and white pepper, or a few dashes of
    hot sauce.
4. Heat carefully, stirring, then add onions and stir
    gently to coat with sauce.

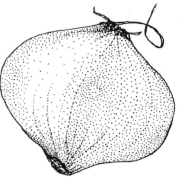

Onion pie

1. Prepare one of the pie crusts on pages 191-193.
2. Preheat oven to 350°
3. Slice about 6 cups of onions and prepare as for creamed onions.
4. Place in crust and bake about 40 minutes.

Eight-Vegetable Pie

one 2-lb eggplant, peeled and thinly sliced
3 cups sliced mushrooms
½ cup finely chopped onion, scallion, or shallot
2 cloves garlic, pressed or finely chopped
2 cups each grated summer squash and grated carrot
2 tblsp sea vegetables (optional)
¼ cup finely chopped fresh parsley
1 tsp basil
¼ tsp tarragon
freshly ground black pepper
1 large ripe tomato

1. Steam eggplant slices until soft. Form an eggplant base in a nonstick or lightly oiled 9-inch pie pan or quiche pan, by placing the slices up around the sides and overlapping them.
2. Preheat oven to 400°.
3. Sauté mushrooms in a small amount of water in a skillet until browned. Spread evenly over eggplant.
4. In the same skillet, sauté onions and garlic briefly, add summer squash, carrot (and sea vegetables), and stir-fry for 3-4 minutes. Season with herbs and pepper. Spread mixture over mushrooms.
5. Cut the tomato in half and slice each half. Place slices around pan to form a border.
6. Bake, covered, about 15 minutes.

Baked Vegetable Chips

1. Slice parsnips, carrots, potatoes, sweet potatoes, kohlrabi, or breadfruit into rounds or sticks. Steam just until tender.
2. Place on a nonstick or lightly oiled baking sheet. Bake at 375° until beginning to crisp, about 10 minutes on one side and 5 on the other.
3. Munch on plain or dip in sauce, such as salsa, ketchup (p. 154), ketchup-like sauce (p. 134), miso sauce (p. 136), or cranberry condiment (p. 155).

BAKED VEGETABLES

potatoes, peeled and cut in quarters lengthwise
onions, left whole, cut in half, or quartered, depending on size
sweet potatoes, peeled and quartered
carrots, peeled or scrubbed, and quartered
garlic cloves, peeled or unpeeled
zucchini or yellow crookneck squash, quartered
celery seeds and dried rosemary

1. Preheat over to 325°.
2. Arrange vegetables in one layer on one or more nonstick baking sheets.
3. Sprinkle liberally with celery seeds and rosemary.
4. Pour a small amount of water on the pan(s). Bake for 35-40 minutes.
Notes: Other vegetables, such as bell peppers, broccoli stems, green beans, kohlrabi, mushrooms, parsnips, rutabagas, and turnips can be added or substituted. And, these can also be baked over a grill (cover the baking sheet with the grill cover) or campfire (cover the sheet with a second, inverted pan).

VEG KEBABS

Light a campfire or charcoal grill and let burn down to hot coals.
Meanwhile, steam briefly over boiling water, just to get the rawness out of them, any vegetables that can be skewered and won't fall apart, such as:

peeled, chunked potatoes or sweet potatoes
peeled, small whole onions or quartered larger ones
scrubbed or peeled and chunked carrots
whole mushrooms
chunked summer squash
large garlic cloves
quartered or eighthed kohlrabi

1. Alternate on skewers, along with pineapple chunks, small green or red tomatoes, and/or cubed tempeh or extra-firm or pressed (p. 6) tofu.
2. Place kebabs on grill over hot coals, or over a gas or electric grill set on low, then rotate slowly until all sides are roasted.
3. These can also be broiled or baked in your kitchen oven.
The vegetables are good as is, or dipped in a miso-based sauce (p. 136) or a tamari-based sauce, such as teriyaki (p. 132), lemon-tamari (p. 138), or tofu dipping sauce (p. 136).

BAKE OUT

1. Light a campfire or charcoal grill and let it burn down to hot coal (or use a gas grill on low setting).
2. Meanwhile, wrap everything in tin foil. If you're careful, you can rinse, dry, and reuse the tin foil for your next bake out. When it's too worn out to use, it can be recycled with metals.
3. Work with the campfire like a grill. Place the wrapped potatoes closely around the hot coals for about ten minutes. Then place all the other vegetables on a grate above the coals, covered with a sheet of lightweight aluminum or galvanized flashing. With a tongs or stick, rotate the position and placement of the potatoes and other vegetables every few minutes for even baking. Bake until the vegetables feel soft and their aromas fill the air. The potatoes take about 45 minutes, depending on size, and the others 10-15 minutes less.
4. The baked vegetables are wonderful as is, or you can enjoy them, especially the potatoes, with some or all of these condiments: freshly ground black pepper, hot sauce, dried parsley, chopped chives, and tamari.

potatoes: Scrub if new, otherwise peel. Wrap large ones individually, or 3-4 small ones in groups.

onions: Cut off as little as possible of the top and bottom. There's no need to peel; the skins will come right off when baked. Wrap large ones singly, and small ones in groups. You won't believe how sweet onions are when cooked this way.

carrots: Cut lengthwise into sticks. (Cut longer ones in half crosswise first.) Divide into groups and double-wrap, or the sharp edges will puncture the tin foil.

mushrooms: Wrap several together.

garlic: Wrap a whole head. Garlic tastes much milder when baked, and the skins come right off.

corn: Remove the outermost husks. Peel down the inner husks just enough to remove the silks. Replace the husks and wrap.

summer squash: Use nice, small ones. Cut in quarters lengthwise, then put the pieces back together and wrap.

These are the standard bake-out vegetables, but the following also work well: pieces of bell pepper, kohlrabi cut in quarters or eighths, tomatoes in a tinfoil pie pan and covered with tin foil, wedges of winter squash and cabbage, and eggplant, cut lengthwise into quarters or into smaller pieces. Tough broccoli stems, saved when you use the florets, soften right up and taste delicious cooked this way.

Note: The vegetables can also be baked-out on a baking sheet. See "baked vegetables" on page 170.

SIMPLER VEGETABLE DISHES

ASPARAGUS

Cut tough, woody ends off the freshest possible asparagus. Place the spears in a steamer over boiling water. Cover and steam just a few minutes, until asparagus is bright green. Eat immediately, plain or with lemon and/or hot sauce.

BEETS

Slice and steam over boiling water until crisp-tender. Serve with lemon.

SPICED CARROTS IN PINEAPPLE JUICE

2 cups sliced, diced, or julienned carrots	¾ tsp cinnamon
¾ cup pineapple juice or crushed pineapple	⅛ tsp nutmeg

Combine all ingredients in a saucepan. Bring to a boil, reduce heat, cover, and simmer about 10 minutes, until carrots are crisp-tender.

BASIL (OR NUTMEG) CARROTS (AND CELERY)

3 cups prepared carrots (see below)
2 cups prepared celery (optional; see below)
1 tblsp chopped fresh, or ½ tsp dried, basil, or ¼ tsp nutmeg
freshly ground black pepper

1. To prepare the vegetables, either cut them diagonally into thin slices or cut them into matchsticks: first cut lengthwise into approximately ¼-inch-diameter strips, then into 1½-inch lengths.
2. Bring a small amount of water to a boil. Reduce heat, add carrots (and celery) and basil, cover and steam over low heat for about 10 minutes, until carrots are tender. Toss with basil or nutmeg, and pepper.

Garden Carrots, Kohlrabi, and Radishes

1. Wash and slice tender young carrots. Slice tender young radishes. Peel and slice kohlrabi, then cut into quarter-rounds.
2. Steam together over boiling water until just beginning to soften.

Good plain or with a dash of tamari.

Fresh Sweet Corn

As you husk the corn, as local and recently picked as possible, boil about ½ inch water in a large wide pan with a flat steamer and lid. (Or you can stand the ears up in ½ inch water in a taller soup pot.) Cover and steam over medium-high heat just until thoroughly, piping hot.

If the corn is very, very fresh, it tastes like candy as is. If it's not quite so fresh and sweet, you can sprinkle it with freshly ground black pepper and/or hot sauce. Sweet corn is best savored as an annual treat during its late-summer, early-fall season.

Greens
Beet Tops, Bok Choy, Chinese cabbage, Collards, Kale, Mustard, Spinach, Swiss Chard, Etc.

1. Wash the greens, but don't dry them. Cut off and compost tough stems, then cut the leaves and chop the more tender stems.
2. Sauté garlic in a small amount of water briefly, then add the greens. Toss, cover, and steam 5-6 minutes, until greens are limp. Sprinkle with lemon juice and/or hot sauce.

Mushrooms

mushrooms	paprika
sliced or chopped onions	chopped fresh or dried parsley

1. To clean mushrooms, wipe them with a dry cloth or use a mushroom brush.
2. Cut off stem ends and slice.
3. Sauté onions in a small amount of water until soft. Sprinkle on paprika and stir in parsley and sliced mushrooms.
4. Cover and steam about 5 minutes, stirring occasionally, until mushrooms are fairly soft.

Parsnips (or Turnips or Rutabagas)

parsnips, turnips, or rutabagas	carrots
finely chopped garlic and grated fresh ginger root or dried ginger or finely chopped onions and a dash of allspice or nutmeg	

1. Cut parsnips, turnips, or rutabagas and carrots into attractive shapes.
2. Sauté in a small amount of water with garlic and ginger until crisp-tender.
3. *Or*, water-sauté with onions and toss with allspice or nutmeg.

Others

Prepare and steam fresh vegetables solo or in infinitely varied combinations.

DESSERT

COOKIES

BARS

CAKES

CRISPS, CRUNCHES, AND COBBLERS

PIE CRUSTS, PIES, TURNOVERS, AND TARTS

PUDDINGS

TOPPINGS

FRUIT DESSERTS

FROZEN DESSERTS

These dessert recipes use brown rice syrup (and/or fruit or fruit juice) as sweetener. Rice syrup can be thinned with orange juice.

Barley malt syrup, brown rice syrup powder, apple fiber powder, and date sugar can be substituted, if you can find and afford them. With some effort, you can make your own date sugar: Bake unfloured "dry" date pieces in a low oven until completely desiccated and brittle. Allow to cool, then pulverize in a food processor.

Each recipe suggests a minimum amount of sweetener. This way, everyone is happy: Those who prefer a less-sweet dessert will like it as is, and those who like it sweeter can spoon on more rice syrup.

The liquid from soaked dried fruit can be used in place of fresh fruit juice.

"Crunchy wheat and barley cereal" refers to generic Grape-Nuts.

Spelt flour can be substituted for whole wheat flour, with excellent results.

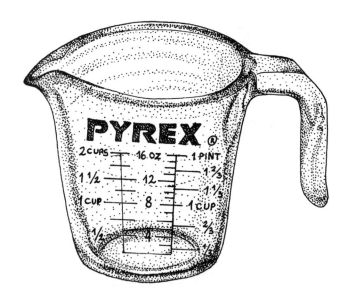

COOKIES

CAROB CHIP KOOKIES

about 12

¾ cup whole wheat pastry flour
½ cup unsweetened carob chips
¼ tsp baking soda
¼ cup crunchy wheat and
   barley cereal (optional)

⅓ cup orange juice (or any fruit juice)
½ tsp vanilla extract
¼ tsp almond extract
2 tblsp rice syrup
raisins, currants, or berries, and/or carob
   powder (optional, see below)

1. Preheat oven to 375°.
2. In a small bowl, mix the flour, carob chips, baking soda, (and cereal).
3. Mix separately the juice—use a bit extra if you're including cereal—
   and extracts (a one-cup liquid measuring cup makes it easy).
4. Pour liquid into dry ingredients. Add rice syrup, and mix quickly, just until the
   dry becomes wet.
5. Place by tablespoon on a nonstick or lightly oiled baking sheet.
6. Bake about 8 minutes—check for bottoms to be nicely browned.

*Raisins or currants and/or 1-2 tblsp carob powder can be added to the dry
ingredients, or berries when you mix it all up. For fudge-like cookies, omit the
baking soda.*

OAT-RICE FLOUR COOKIES

about 16-20

¾ cup brown rice flour
1 cup rolled oats
½ tsp baking soda
½ tsp cinnamon

½ cup orange juice
¼ cup rice syrup
½ cup raisins or currants

1. Preheat oven to 400°.
2. Combine flour, oats, soda, and cinnamon. Add orange juice and rice syrup;
   mix well. Fold in raisins.
3. Drop by teaspoon or tablespoon onto a nonstick or lightly oiled baking sheet.
4. Bake 8-10 minutes, until bottoms are nicely browned.

Oat-Spice Cookies

about 12-16

½ cup whole wheat pastry flour	1/ tsp ginger
1 cup rolled oats	¼ tsp allspice
½ tsp baking powder	½ cup orange, apple, or other fruit juice
½ tsp cinnamon	2-4 tblsp rice syrup
¼ tsp cloves	¼ cup raisins or currants

1. Preheat oven to 375°.
2. Combine flour, oats, baking powder and spices.
3. Add juice and rice syrup and mix well. Fold in raisins.
4. Drop by teaspoons or tablespoon onto a nonstick or lightly oiled baking sheet.
5. Bake 8-10 minutes, until bottoms are nicely browned.

Simplest Applesauce-Oat Cookies

about 16

¾ cup applesauce (p. 207) or grated apple	2 cups rolled oats
2 tblsp rice syrup	¼ cup chopped dates
½ tsp vanilla	

1. Preheat oven to 375°.
2. Combine all ingredients.
3. Drop by tablespoon onto a nonstick or lightly oiled baking sheet.
4. Bake about 15 minutes or until well browned.

A Bit More Complex Applesauce-Oat Cookies

about 18

1. Preheat oven to 350°.
2. Combine dry ingredients in a medium bowl:

½ cup whole wheat pastry flour	¼ tsp baking soda
⅔ cup rolled oats	¼ tsp cinnamon
½ tsp baking powder	¼ cup carob chips (optional)

Combine in a small bowl:

½ cup applesauce (p. 185) or other fruit sauce, or grated apple	½ tsp vanilla
2 tblsp rice syrup	¼ cup raisins or currants
	¼ cup chopped dates (optional)

1. Add wet to dry and mix well.
2. Drop by tablespoon onto a nonstick or lightly oiled baking sheet.
3. Bake about 10 minutes, until bottoms are well browned.

Carrot-Date Mini-cakes
about 20

1 cup whole wheat pastry flour	1 cup chopped pitted dates
¼ cup crunchy wheat and barley cereal	1 cup grated carrots
¼ tsp baking soda	2 tblsp rice syrup
⅛ tsp each allspice and nutmeg	¼ cup orange juice
(or ¾-1 tsp ginger and ⅛-³⁄₁₆ tsp cloves)	1 tsp vanilla

1. Preheat oven to 350°.
2. Combine flour, cereal, baking soda, and spices.
3. Combine the remaining ingredients in a larger bowl, or purée in a processor.
4. Stir dry ingredients into date mixture, just until blended.
5. Drop by heaping tablespoon onto a nonstick or lightly oiled baking sheet.
6. Bake about 15 minutes, until bottoms are nicely browned.

Halvah Cookies
about 12 large or 24 bite-size

½ cup tahini	2 cups rolled oats (soft, baby, or quick are best)
4-6 tblsp rice syrup	raisins or currants (optional)
¼ cup + 1 tblsp orange juice	

1. Preheat the oven to 350°.
2. Stir the tahini, rice syrup, and orange juice together until well blended.
3. Stir in the oats. Mix raisins with all or some of the batter.
4. Drop by tablespoon onto a nonstick or lightly oiled baking sheet.
5. Bake 10 minutes, until bottoms are nicely browned.

Tofu-Brown Rice Cookies
about 18

12 oz tofu, squeezed (p. 6)	¼ cup raisins or currants
1 cup cooked brown rice (p. 2)	cinnamon
¼ cup rice syrup	

1. Preheat oven to 350°.
2. Combine tofu, rice, rice syrup, and raisins; mix well. Form into small patties and place on a nonstick or lightly oiled baking sheet. Sprinkle with cinnamon.
3. Bake 15-20 minutes, until nicely browned.

Cinnamon-Raisin Dessert Biscuits

Follow the recipe for cinnamon biscuits on p. 37, with these changes: Use whole wheat pastry flour instead of bread flour, and add raisins or currants to the batter.

BARS

DRIED-FRUIT BARS

1 cup whole wheat pastry flour
¼ tsp baking powder
⅜ cup orange juice
2-4 tblsp rice syrup
1 cup chopped dried fruit, such as dates, prunes, or apricots
  (chop in food processor)*

1. Preheat oven to 350°.
2. Combine flour and baking powder. Add orange juice, rice syrup, and chopped
   dried fruit. Mix well.
3. Spread in a nonstick or lightly oiled 8-inch square or 9-inch round baking pan.
4. Bake about 20 minutes.
*These can be "plumped" (soaked or heated in water or juice) first and the liquid used
   as fruit juice in this or any recipe.

OAT-FRUIT BARS

2 cups whole wheat pastry flour
2 cups rolled oats
1 cup orange juice
2 tblsp rice syrup
2 tblsp each lemon or lime juice and rice syrup
1 cup applesauce or grated raw apple
1 cup chopped dates* (see note above)
1 cup raisins or currants* (see note above)

1. Preheat oven to 400°.
2. Combine flour, oats, orange juice, and 2 tblsp rice syrup.
3. Press half the mixture into a nonstick or lightly oiled 13- by 9-inch baking pan.
4. In a saucepan combine the lemon or lime juice and the remaining 2 tblsp rice
   syrup. Add applesauce, dates, and raisins.
5. Cook and stir over low heat about 10 minutes. Cool slightly and spread over
   mixture in pan.
6. Crumble the rest of the oat mix over all. Bake 20 to 30 minutes.

Sweet Oatcakes

3 cups rolled oats
¾ cup vanilla soymilk
¾ cup orange juice
¼ cup rice syrup

1 tsp almond extract
½ cup raisins or currants
½ tsp cinnamon
applesauce, grated apple, or drained
   crushed pineapple (optional)

1. Combine all ingredients. Let sit 30 minutes.
2. Preheat oven to 400°.
3. Spread in a nonstick or lightly oiled 12- by 14-inch baking pan.
4. Bake 20-25 minutes.

Quantums

1 cup currants or raisins
1 cup boiling water
1¼ cups whole wheat pastry flour
1 tsp baking soda
1 tsp cinnamon

½ cup applesauce (p. 207),
   other fruit sauce, or grated raw apple
2-4 tblsp rice syrup
1 tsp lemon juice
1 tsp vanilla extract
¼ tsp almond extract

1. Preheat oven to 350°.
2. In a small bowl, combine currants and water; let stand 30 minutes.
3. In another small bowl, combine flour, baking soda, and cinnamon.
4. In a larger bowl, combine applesauce, lemon juice, rice syrup, and extracts.
5. When currants are plumped (reserve liquid for another use), add to applesauce mixture, then stir in dry ingredients and mix well.
6. Place batter in a 9-inch square pan. Bake about 30 minutes.

Carob Brownies - Chewy

1 cup whole wheat pastry flour
6 tblsp carob powder
1 tsp baking powder
½ cup chopped roasted chestnuts (p. 213) (optional)

½ cup vanilla soymilk
2 tblsp rice syrup
½ cup raisins or currants

1. Preheat oven to 350°.
2. Combine flour, carob, and baking powder.
3. Quickly stir in soymilk, rice syrup, raisins or currants, and chestnuts, stirring just enough to moisten.
4. Spoon into a nonstick or lightly oiled 8-inch square or 9-inch round baking pan and spread evenly.
5. Bake about 15 minutes.

CAROB BROWNIES - CAKEY

1 cup whole wheat pastry flour	½ cup applesauce
¼ cup carob powder	2 tblsp rice syrup
1 tsp baking powder	1 tsp vanilla
½ cup chopped roasted chestnuts (p. 213) (optional)	

1. Preheat oven to 325°.
2. Combine dry ingredients; combine wet ingredients separately.
3. Add dry to wet and mix briefly but thoroughly.
4. Spread in a nonstick or lightly oiled 8-inch square baking pan.
5. Bake 15-20 minutes.

BROWNIE PUDDING

Place pieces of brownie in a bowl, top with berries or other fruit if you like, pour vanilla soymilk over, and eat with a spoon.

CAROB-TOFU FUDGE

6-8 oz tofu	¼ cup rice syrup
4 tsp carob powder	1 tsp vanilla extract
½ cup whole wheat pastry flour	½ cup unsweetened carob chips
⅛ tsp cinnamon	½ cup chopped roasted chestnuts (p. 213) (optional)

1. Preheat oven to 350°.
2. Purée tofu in a blender or food processor.
3. Add carob powder, flour, and cinnamon and blend 30 seconds.
4. Add rice syrup and vanilla and blend 30 seconds.
5. Add carob chips and blend 30 seconds. Briefly blend in chopped chestnuts.
6. Place in nonstick or lightly oiled and flour-dusted 8-inch square baking pan.
7. Bake 15 minutes.

CAKES

Because these cakes contain no shortening or eggs, and a minimum of baking
soda or baking powder (which inhibit complete assimilation of nutrients in the
other ingredients), they are more dense, moist, and chewy than cakes made
with fat, cholesterol, and excessive non-yeast leavening agents.

You can make a double batch and stack them to make a layer cake. Or slice one
cake laterally to make two layers. Let the cake cool, then fill and ice with a
tofu- or fruit-based topping (p. 202-203).

APPLESAUCE CAKE

1½ cups whole wheat pastry flour
½ tsp baking soda
1 tsp cinnamon
½ tsp ground cloves

1 cup applesauce (p. 207)
2-4 tblsp rice syrup
1 cup raisins

1. Preheat oven to 350°.
2. Combine flour, baking soda, and spices. Add applesauce, rice syrup,
   and raisins.
3. Mix well.
4. Bake in a nonstick or lightly oiled 8-inch square or 9-inch round cake pan
   for 35 to 40 minutes.

UNLEAVENED SPICE AND RAISIN CAKE

1¼ cups grain beverage (p. 217)
¼ cup barley malt syrup or rice syrup
2 cups whole wheat pastry flour
3 tblsp carob powder
¼ tsp each cinnamon, nutmeg, and allspice

1 tsp vanilla
¼ tsp almond extract
¼ cup grated apple
   (or apple fiberpowder)
1 cup raisins

1. Preheat oven to 350°.
2. Boil water and prepare grain beverage. Stir in syrup to dissolve. Let cool.
3. Meanwhile, combine flour, carob, and spices (and apple powder)
   in a medium bowl.
4. Stir vanilla and almond extract into liquid. Pour into dry ingredients and mix.
   Add grated apple and raisins and mix well.
5. Use a rubber spatula to transfer the batter to a nonstick or lightly oiled 9-inch
   square pan. Moisten the spatula to help smooth the surface of the cake.
6. Bake 30-35 minutes.

CARROT CAKE

Use Carrot Muffin recipe on page 35. Pour batter into two nonstick or lightly oiled 9-inch round cake pans and bake 45 minutes.

SHORTCAKE

2 cups whole wheat pastry flour	¾ cup vanilla soymilk
1½ tsp baking powder	2 tblsp rice syrup
fruit and topping (see below)	

1. Preheat oven to 350°.
2. Combine flour and baking powder. Add soymilk and rice syrup and mix quickly, just enough to dampen the dry ingredients thoroughly.
3. Spread in a nonstick or lightly oiled 9-inch round or 8-inch square baking pan. Bake about 15 minutes.
4. Cut shortcake into squares and split open. Top with berries, chopped peaches, other fruit, or fruit sauce (p. 207), and soy yogurt (p. 10), tofu whipped cream (p. 202), tofu-fruit whip (p. 202), or banana-sesame cream (p. 202).

UPSIDE-DOWN CAKE

Place unsweetened pineapple rings, or other sliced fruit, on the bottom of the pan before pouring in the batter. After baking, allow to cool, then use a nonstick utensil to loosen cake around the edges, place a plate over the pan, and invert.

GINGER BARS OR SHORTCAKE

2 cups whole wheat pastry flour	¼ tsp ground cloves
1 tsp baking powder	¼-½ cup barley malt syrup
1½ -2 tsp each ground ginger and cinnamon	1 cup vanilla soymilk

1. Preheat oven to 350°
2. Combine flour, baking powder, and spices in a bowl.
3. Heat barley malt and soymilk just until blended. Pour into dry ingredients and mix well.
4. Spread in a nonstick or lightly oiled 9-inch square baking pan. Bake about 30 minutes.
5. This cake can be eaten plain, or split open and topped with rice syrup, berries or other chopped fruit, and/or tofu whipped cream (p. 202), tofu-fruit whip (p. 202), or banana-sesame cream (p. 202).

CORN-SPICE-RAISIN CAKE

1 cup cornmeal
1 cup whole wheat pastry flour, or
    ¾ cup pastry flour and ¼ cup brown rice flour
1 tsp baking powder
½ tsp each cinnamon and nutmeg
1 cup total orange juice and/or vanilla soymilk
2-4 tblsp rice syrup
1 cup raisins

1. Preheat oven to 350°.
2. Combine cornmeal, flour, baking powder, and spices in a bowl.
3. Add liquid and rice syrup and mix well. Stir in raisins.
4. Transfer to a nonstick or lightly oiled 9-inch round baking pan and
   bake about 30 minutes.
5. An applesauce-soy yogurt blend makes a good sauce for this cake.

FRUIT CAKE

1¾ cups whole wheat pastry flour   ½ cup orange juice
1½ tsp baking powder   ½ cup vanilla soymilk
½ tsp cinnamon   ½ tsp almond extract
    2 tblsp rice syrup
1 cup total: cranberries, raisins, currants, berries; chopped dried fruit, such as apricots,
    dates, prunes; chopped fresh fruit, such as apples, peaches, nectarines, plums;
    or ½-¾ cup poppy seeds

1. Preheat oven to 350°.
2. Combine flour, baking powder, and cinnamon.
3. Separately, mix the remaining ingredients.
4. Add wet to dry, mix well, spread in 8- or 9-inch square pan.
5. Bake 30-45 minutes, until toothpick inserted in the center comes out clean.

TOFU CHEESECAKE

Crust

½ cup rolled oats	2 tblsp rice syrup
½ cup crunchy wheat and barley cereal	1 tblsp lemon or other fruit juice

Filling

20 oz firm or extra-firm tofu	½ tsp grated lemon rind
¼ cup rice syrup 2 tblsp tahini	
1 tblsp lemon juice or other fruit juice	½ tsp vanilla

1. Preheat oven to 350°.
2. Combine crust ingredients and press into a nonstick or lightly oiled 8-inch pie pan.
3. Purée filling ingredients in a blender or processor and spoon into crust. Smooth filling surface.
4. Bake about 35 minutes or until surface is lightly browned. Let cool.
5. You can decorate the cake with sliced strawberries, kiwifruit, and/or other fruit.

Fruity Options

Decrease tofu to 16 oz and add 2-4 ripe bananas or 2 cups well-drained finely chopped fresh or crushed canned pineapple.

FOUR-LAYER APRICOT-TOFU CHEESECAKE

Prepare crust and filling for Tofu Cheesecake (above). Reserve one cup filling.

Prepare apricot topping:

2 cups dried apricots
¼ tsp cinnamon
¼ tsp nutmeg

1. Cook apricots in water to cover for ½ hour. Purée with spices in blender or processor.
2. Purée 1 cup apricot topping with the reserved cup of tofu filling.
3. Spoon the remaining tofu filling over crust, then pour the apricot-tofu mixture over the tofu filling.
4. Bake 45 minutes, or until firm.
5. Cool, then cover with remaining apricot topping.

TORTE

stale cinnamon-raisin bread (p. 42)— 3 slices per torte vanilla soymilk or undiluted concentrate	dried-fruit jam (p. 203) tofu whipped cream (p. 202) berries or other fruit

1. Preheat oven to 250°.
2. Place bread slices on a baking pan and spread soymilk or concentrate on them just until moistened. Turn the slices over and do the same on the other side.
3. Bake slices until dry but still soft, then flip and bake a few more minutes.
4. To assemble: Spread one slice with dried-fruit jam and tofu whipped cream; top with fresh fruit. Repeat for the second and third slices.
5. Cut in half diagonally and serve.

CRISPS, CRUNCHES, AND COBBLERS

APPLE OR PEAR CRISP

6-8 cups apples and/or pears, cut into bite-sized pieces
¾-1 cup raisins or currants
2-3 cups rolled oats
¾-1 cup whole wheat flour
½-1 tsp cinnamon
1½ cups apple juice, orange juice, or other juice
topping: soy yogurt (p. 10), tofu whipped cream (p. 202),
banana-sesame cream (p. 202), or tofu-fruit whip (p. 202)

1. Spread apples in a nonstick or lightly oiled 9-inch square or 9- by 12-inch baking pan. Add raisins or currants.
2. Mix oats, flour, and cinnamon. Cover apples and lightly pat down.
3. Slowly pour apple juice over. Let sit 20-30 minutes. Preheat oven to 350°.
4. Bake 20-25 minutes, until crust browns. If you like, serve with one of the toppings.

Any-fruit Crisp

Substitute any of the Fruit Crunch filling combinations (p. 191) for the
apples or pears.

Fruit Crunch

Crust

½ cup whole wheat pastry flour	2-4 tblsp rice syrup
1 cup rolled oats	½ cup orange juice

1. Preheat the oven to 375°.
2. Combine crust ingredients. Press half of the mixture into a nonstick or lightly oiled 9-inch pan.
3. Place filling ingredients over crust mixture in baking pan.
4. Place remaining crust mixture on fruit. Bake 45 minutes, until filling is bubbly and crust is browned.
5. Serve plain or topped with soy yogurt (p. 10), tofu whipped cream (p. 202), tofu-fruit whip (p. 202), or banana-sesame cream (p. 202).

Fillings

rhubarb: Combine 3-4 cups rhubarb, cut into ½-inch slices, with ¼ cup rice syrup and 2 tblsp granulated tapioca.

strawberry-rhubarb: Substitute sliced strawberries for some of the rhubarb; reduce sweetener.

strawberry-apple: Use 3-4 cups total sliced strawberries and chopped apples.

blueberry: Mix 2-3 cups blueberries, 1/8 tsp nutmeg, and 1 tblsp granulated tapioca.

cranberry: Place 1 pound of cranberries in a saucepan. Cook until they pop and then 1 or 2 minutes longer, without letting them get mushy. Sweeten with rice syrup. Cool slightly.

any berry or stonefruit: Use berries straight from bush or container, and/or slice or chop peaches, nectarines, plums, and/or apricots for a total of 3-4 cups.

CRANBERRY-APPLE COBBLER

3 large apples, cut into small pieces
   2 cups cranberries
2 tsp almond extract
¼ cup rice syrup
grated rind of 1 lemon

1 cup total wheat germ, bran, and/or
   crunchy wheat and barley cereal
1 tsp cinnamon
½ tsp kelp powder (optional)

1. Preheat oven to 375°.
2. Combine apples, cranberries, almond extract, rice syrup, and lemon rind.
   Place in a nonstick or lightly oiled 1½-2 quart baking dish.
3. Combine the wheat germ/bran/cereal, cinnamon, and kelp, and sprinkle over
   the fruit mixture.
4. Bake 45 minutes, until bubbly and brown.

Cranberry Crunch and Cranberry-Apple Cobbler Combination
Use the crunch crust and cranberry-apple cobbler fruit mix filling.

PIE CRUSTS, PIES, TURNOVERS, AND TARTS

Note on pie crusts and pies: The crusts, made with a minimum of fat, aren't as
flaky as conventional crusts. All the crusts and pies are 9-inch.

INSTANT PRESSED PIE CRUST (9-INCH)

When you need pastry for a one-crust pie, this is the one to use. Doubled, you
can use it for a two-crust or lattice pie: press in the bottom and roll out the top.

1¼ cups whole wheat pastry flour
2 tblsp sesame oil
6 tblsp (¼ cup + 2 tblsp) boiling water

1. Measure flour into a bowl. Add boiling water to oil and beat with a fork.
2. Pour into flour and mix well until dough holds together in a ball.
3. Place dough in the center of a nonstick or lightly oiled pie pan and press
   evenly into place. Flute edge.

WHOLE WHEAT PIE CRUST (9-INCH)

1 cup whole wheat pastry flour*
2 tblsp sesame oil
about 3 tblsp ice water

Substituting wheat gluten for some of the flour will make the dough more pliable and easier to work with, but tougher when baked.

1. Put flour in a small bowl. Stir in oil and enough water to make a very stiff dough.
2. Roll out on a floured board to an 11- to 12-inch circle and fit into a nonstick or lightly oiled pie pan.
3. Turn under the edge and flute.
4. Double the recipe for a two-crust or lattice pie.

WHOLE WHEAT-RICE PIE CRUST (9-INCH)

½ cup whole wheat pastry flour   2 tblsp sesame oil
½ cup brown rice flour   about 3 tblsp ice water

1. Put flour in a small bowl. Stir in oil and enough water to make a very stiff dough.
2. Roll out on a floured board to an 11- to 12-inch circle and fit into a nonstick or lightly oiled pie pan.
3. Turn the edge under and flute.
4. Double the recipe for a two-crust or lattice pie.

PRESS-IN OAT PIE CRUST (9-INCH)

1 cup soft rolled oats   ½ cup whole wheat pastry flour
water

1. Combine oats and flour. Add enough water to make a moist but not sticky dough.
2. Pat into a nonstick or lightly oiled pie pan.

CRUNCHY PRESS-IN PIE CRUST (9-INCH)

1½ cups crunchy wheat and barley cereal*   ¼ cup rice syrup
½ cup rolled oats   ⅓ cup orange juice

1. Combine ingredients and press on bottom and sides of a nonstick or lightly oiled pie pan.
2. For a no-cook pie, bake at 375° for 8 minutes before filling.

For a finer crust, grind the cereal in a blender or food processor to make tiny, powdery crumbs. Use small, soft rolled oats, or grind larger or harder rolled oats with the cereal.

MILLET OR AMARANTH CRUST

¼ cup rolled oats or ground sunflower and/or pumpkin seeds
3 tblsp instant tapioca granules
⅔ cup raw millet or amaranth, rinsed in a sieve
½ cup apple juice or water

Combine oats or ground seeds, millet or amaranth, and tapioca in a small bowl. Bring juice or water to a boil in a small pot, pour over dry ingredients, stir well, and cover. Let sit while you prepare filling. Then place mixture in a nonstick or lightly oiled pie pan and use a spatula to spread it evenly over the bottom and sides.

APPLE PIE

pastry for 2-crust pie (p. 191) for sliced apples,
  or millet or amaranth crust (above) for chopped apples
4-6 cups sliced or finely chopped tart apples*   2 tblsp orange juice
  (Wild apples are best!)   ½ tsp cinnamon
2-4 tblsp rice syrup   1½ tblsp whole wheat flour or
                                                    arrowroot powder

*A food processor works well for both slicing and chopping the apples.

1. Preheat the oven to 400°.
2. Combine filling ingredients. Place in pie shell.
3. For a double crust, place top crust over, seal edges, and decorate. Make steam slashes.
4. Bake 40-50 minutes until filling is tender and crust is slightly browned. Cover pie with tin foil or an inverted pie tin if it begins to over-brown.

Apple-Cranberry Pie

Substitute:

1 cup fresh or frozen cranberries, or ½ cup chopped dried cranberries,
    for 1 cup of sliced apples

Pear Pie

Use 4-5 cups of cut-up pears. Add ¼ tsp nutmeg. If the pears are very juicy,
    omit orange juice.

APPLE-APPLESAUCE PIE

crunchy press-in pie shell (p. 192)
2 cups thick homemade applesauce (can be spiced and sweetened)
2 cups thinly sliced peeled apple rings
½ cup apricot jam (p. 203)
½ cup orange juice

1. Preheat oven to 425°.
2. Spoon applesauce into pie shell. Place apple rings on applesauce in slightly
   overlapping circles.
3. Combine jam and juice in a small pan, heat and stir until well blended, then
   spread over apple rings.
4. Sprinkle with ½ cup crunchy wheat and barley cereal.
5. Bake about 25 minutes, until apple rings are tender.

Pineapple-Apple Pie

Substitute:

1-2 cups well-drained crushed pineapple for some or all of the applesauce.

You could use the drained pineapple juice in place of the orange juice.

PUMPKIN PIE

single-crust pie shell (p. 191-193) or tofu cheesecake crust (p. 188)
3 cups pumpkin purée (p. 161)
⅓ - ½ cup rice syrup
2 tblsp kanten flakes or agar, arrowroot or kuzu (see p. 13), or cornstarch
    or granulated tapioca
1 cup vanilla soymilk
1 tsp cinnamon
¼ tsp ground ginger
1⁄16-⅛ tsp ground cloves and/or nutmeg

1. Preheat oven to 350°.
2. Blend filling ingredients in a food processor, or beat together in a bowl.
3. Pour into pie shell and bake 50-60 minutes, or until a tester inserted in
    the center comes out clean.

FRESH BERRY PIE

pastry for lattice pie (p. 191)
2 tblsp cornstarch (or arrowroot or kuzu: see p. 13)
2 tblsp lemon juice
2 tblsp rice syrup
5-6 cups blueberries, raspberries, black raspberries, or blackberries

1. Preheat oven to 400°.
2. Dissolve thickener in lemon juice; stir in rice syrup. Toss with berries.
3. Transfer to pie shell and cover with lattice.
4. Bake about 45 minutes, until crust is golden brown and fruit is bubbly.

Peach Pie

Toss 5-6 cups sliced ripe peaches with lemon juice, rice syrup, and a dash of
    cinnamon and nutmeg.

RAISIN-APPLE PIE

pastry for lattice pie (p. 191)
¼ cup rice syrup
2 tblsp cornstarch
  (or arrowroot or kuzu; see p. 13)
½ tsp cinnamon
¼ tsp nutmeg

2 cups cranberry-apple juice or other fruit juice
  or combination
2 cups raisins
½ tsp almond extract
2 cups sliced apples

1. Preheat oven to 450°.
2. Combine rice syrup, thickener, cinnamon, and nutmeg in a saucepan.
3. Blend in juice. Add raisins and cook over low heat, stirring constantly, until thick and clear. Add almond extract. Cool slightly.
4. Line pie shell with sliced apples. Pour in raisin mixture and cover with lattice.
5. Bake at 450° for 10 minutes, then lower heat to 350° and bake 20 more minutes, until pastry is golden brown.

"You Can't Have Too Many Raisins" Pie

Omit apples. Instead, use a total of 4 cups of raisins.

FRUIT AND TAPIOCA PIE

1. Prepare a pie shell (p. 191-193).
2. Bake at 350° for about 10 minutes, until set and lightly browned. Cool.
3. Line baked crust with sliced bananas, peaches, nectarines; steamed apple rings; drained crushed pineapple and/or other fruit, and fill with cooked tapioca pudding (p. 200).
Or, fill crust with tapioca and cover with berries.
Or, mix tapioca with berries and/or other fruit and fill crust.
4. Refrigerate until firm.

Banana-Carob-Tapioca Pie

Fill crust with very ripe bananas whipped with carob-tapioca pudding (p. 200).

FRUIT AND TOFU PIE

instant pressed crust (p. 191), baked 5 minutes at 350°
4 cups total fruit—singly or in any combination, such as berries;
    sliced peaches, apples, pears; chopped pineapple; sliced rhubarb*
    (Mix rhubarb, which is tart, with some rice syrup.)
tofu whipped cream (p. 202; double the recipe)

Strawberry-rhubarb is a traditional favorite combination.

1. Place fruit in baked crust and top with tofu. Or, layer fruit-tofu-fruit-tofu.
2. Bake at 350° 45 minutes, until fruit bubbles and tofu topping is light brown.

LASSIE BUNS, TURNOVERS, OR CRESCENTS

8-12

3 cups whole wheat pastry flour (add more if needed for a non-sticky dough)
½ tsp each cinnamon, ginger, and allspice
¼ tsp cloves
1½ tsp baking soda
½ cup total rice syrup and/or barley malt syrup
½ cup warm water

Preheat oven to 400°. Mix well, shape, and bake 15 minutes.

Buns

Roll to ½-inch thickness and cut into squares or rectangles.

Turnovers

1. Roll to ¼-inch thickness and cut into 4- to 6-inch squares.
2. Place a tablespoon of jam (p. 204) or turnover filling (p. 198) on one side of
    the square, fold in half, and pinch the edges.
3. For triangles, place the filling toward one corner and fold diagonally.

Crescents

1. Roll to ¼-inch thickness and cut into 4-inch squares.
2. Spread with jam (p. 204) or any puréed filling.
3. Starting at one corner, roll up and bend into a crescent shape.

Turnovers and Tarts

Dough

½ cup each: whole wheat pastry flour, brown rice flour, wheat gluten, soft rolled oats
2 tblsp sesame oil
about ¼ cup cold water

1. Combine flours. Stir in oil and enough cold water to make a pliable but non-sticky dough. Roll out thinly on a floured surface. Press the rim of a bowl or small pot lid into the dough to make 4- to 6-inch circles.
2. Re-roll the trimmings to use all the dough. Or, save lots of time by just cutting the rolled-out dough into 4- to 6-inch squares.
3. Place circles or squares of dough on a nonstick or lightly oiled baking sheet. There should be about 8-12, depending on size.
4. Preheat oven to 350°.
5. For tarts, place a rounded tablespoon of filling in the center of the circle or square and pinch corners together around it to make a four-blade pinwheel. Press down the "blades."
6. For turnovers, place a heaping tablespoon of filling on one side of the circle or square, fold in half, and pinch the edges together. To make triangles, place the filling toward one corner of the square and fold in half diagonally.
7. Bake 20 minutes, until filling is bubbly and dough is lightly browned.

Fillings

Prune

1½ cups cooked pitted prunes	⅛ tsp nutmeg
grated rind of a lemon	½ tsp cinnamon
1-2 tblsp rice syrup	

Purée prunes. Add remaining ingredients.

Poppy seed

1 cup poppy seeds	1 cup orange juice
½ cup raisins	1 tsp vanilla
2-4 tblsp rice syrup	

Combine poppy seeds, raisins, rice syrup, and juice in a pan. Bring to
boiling point, reduce heat, cover, and simmer 10 minutes. Stir in vanilla.
Cool before using.

Apple, apple-cranberry, apple-raisin, or apple-prune

1. Combine 1½ cups of chopped apples with some rice syrup and cinnamon.
2. Coat with a small amount of lemon, lime, or orange juice. Or, reduce the
   amount of apples and add cranberries or plumped raisins, currants, or
   puréed prunes.

Berry, peach, or other fruit or combination

1½ tsp cornstarch	1½ tsp rice syrup
(or arrowroot or kuzu: see p. 13)	1½ cups fruit
1½ tsp lemon or lime juice	

Combine thickener, juice, and rice syrup. Toss with fruit.

PUDDINGS

TAPIOCA PUDDING

3 cups vanilla soymilk   ½ cup small tapioca pearls

1. In a saucepan, soak tapioca in soymilk 15 minutes.
2. Stirring frequently, bring to a boil, then reduce heat to medium and cook 8-10 minutes.
3. Transfer to a bowl and let sit until thick, or chill.

Instant Tapioca Pudding

3 cups vanilla soymilk
4-6 tblsp granulated tapioca, depending on desired firmness

1. In a saucepan, soak tapioca in soymilk 5 minutes.
2. Stirring frequently, bring to a boil, then reduce heat to medium and cook about 1 minute.
3. Cool slightly, then pour into a bowl or serving dishes and chill.

Carob-Tapioca Pudding

1. Use carob soymilk or blend 3 tblsp carob powder with the vanilla soymilk.

TOFU-BROWN RICE PUDDING

8 oz tofu, mashed
3 cups cooked brown rice (p. 2)
1 cup vanilla soymilk
¼ cup rice syrup
¼ cup crunchy wheat and barley cereal

½ tsp cinnamon
¼ cup raisins or chopped dates
other fruit: berries; chopped apples, pineapple, peaches, etc. (optional)

1. Preheat oven to 350°.
2. Combine tofu, rice, soymilk, rice syrup, cinnamon, raisins or dates, and fruit; mix well.
3. Place in a nonstick or lightly oiled bread pan or casserole, sprinkle with cereal, and bake 25 minutes, or until set.

Brown Rice, Couscous, Millet, or Oatmeal Pudding

See page 25.

Oats and Apples Pudding

2 cups rolled oats	3 cups applesauce (p. 207)
¾ cup raisins	2 cups vanilla soymilk
3 cups peeled, cored, and cubed apples	dash cinnamon

1. Mix. If you prefer it hot, mix in a pot and heat through.
2. You can use cooked brown rice, couscous, millet, or other grain in place of the raw oats.

Warm Noodle Pudding

3 cups hot cooked pasta (flats are traditional)	½ cup vanilla soymilk grated rind of ½ lemon or lime
1 cup raisins or currants	⅛ tsp cinnamon
1 cup chopped apple	¼ cup poppy seeds (optional)
2 tblsp rice syrup	

1. Place raisins or currants and chopped apple in a small pot and add enough water to just cover them.
2. Bring to a boil and simmer 10-15 minutes.
3. Drain; save the liquid as juice or to use in another recipe.
4. In a bowl, combine pasta and drained fruit with remaining ingredients.

Quick, Cold Noodle Pudding

Combine cold leftover pasta, raisins or currants, any chopped fresh fruit or combination, and the other noodle pudding ingredients.

Both noodle puddings, warm and cold, are excellent with soy yogurt (p. 10).

TOPPINGS

If you make a double batch of any of the cakes on pages 185-187 or slice one cake laterally to make two layers, you can use these toppings to make a special-occasion layer cake. Let the cake cool, then fill and ice.

TOFU WHIPPED CREAM

8 oz tofu
2 tblsp rice syrup
½ tsp vanilla, or ⅛ tsp almond extract and 3 tblsp tahini

Purée in a blender or food processor, or use soft or silken tofu if blending with a fork.

TOFU-FRUIT WHIP

8 oz tofu
1 cup fruit, such as berries, chopped peaches, bananas, or pineapple
    (Try cranberries with apples and/or pears to top a fall or winter pie.)
2 tblsp rice syrup
¼ tsp vanilla
additional berries or chopped fruit (optional, see below)

1. Purée in a blender or food processor. If you like, stir in more fruit.
2. Eat as pudding or as a topping for other desserts.

BANANA-SESAME CREAM

Purée in a blender or food processor:

4 oz tofu	¼ tsp vanilla, almond extract, or other
1 tblsp rice syrup	natural flavoring; or
1 banana	2 tblsp all-fruit preserves,
1 tblsp tahini	or 1-2 tsp carob powder

60-SECOND CAROB TOPPING OR FONDUE

¼ cup carob powder
¼ cup vanilla soymilk (less for icing)
1 tblsp rice syrup

1. Stir soymilk into carob powder over medium-low heat. Add rice syrup and continue stirring until warm, smooth, and satiny.
2. Use as icing for cake or topping for slices of quick bread or cinnamon-raisin bread.
3. For fondue, transfer the mixture into a small bowl. Cut any kind of fruit and sweet baked thing into large cubes, and experience bliss.

60-SECOND CAROB CHIP TOPPING OR FONDUE

½ cup unsweetened carob chips
2 tblsp vanilla soymilk
2 tblsp rice syrup

Melt ingredients together in a small pan over very low heat.

PINEAPPLE FROTH

Purée fresh or unsweetened canned pineapple—crushed, tidbits, chunks, or rings, and with or without its juice, depending on desired thinness.

DRIED-FRUIT JAM

Any whole or chopped dried fruit or combination can be cooked in fruit juice for about 30 minutes or soaked until soft (at least 2 hours or overnight), then mashed and whipped, or puréed in a blender or food processor until smooth. Spread on bread, toast, crackers, rice cakes, shortcake, etc. It keeps well in a covered container in the refrigerator. Here are some examples.

Orange-Date Jam

1½ cups dates with 2 cups orange juice, and grated orange or lemon rind (optional)

Pineapricot Jam

1½ cups apricots with 2 cups pineapple juice

Apple-Apricot Jam

1½ cups apricots with 2 cups apple juice (and ¼ cup orange juice concentrate, optional)

After cooking or soaking, stir in ½ tsp almond extract and ¼ tsp cinnamon.

BERRY TOPPING

Mash with a fork and whip, or purée in a blender or processor:

blueberries, blackberries, black raspberries, loganberries, raspberries,
    strawberries, or any locally pickable berry delights
rice syrup to taste
small amount lemon or lime juice

APPLE BUTTER

1. If you cook applesauce (p. 207) long enough, it will become apple butter. You
   can also add a sweetener and spices such as cinnamon, cloves, and allspice.
2. Cook it uncovered on a very low heat, stirring often, until it becomes very
   thick, about 2½ hours.
3. Every quart of peeled and sliced or chunked apples will yield about 1½ cups
   of apple butter.

PUMPKIN CONSERVE

about 3 cups

2 cups pumpkin purée (p. 145)	½ cup raisins
½ cup rice syrup or barley malt syrup	¼ tsp allspice
½ cup finely chopped dried apricots,	1 tsp grated lemon or lime rind
papaya, or other dried fruit	1 tblsp lemon or lime juice

1. Combine all ingredients in a saucepan and cook over low heat for about
   40 minutes, stirring often.
2. Store in refrigerator. Or, pour into hot, sterilized half-pint (1-cup) canning jars,
   wipe rims with a clean cloth, cap with sterilized lids and rings, and process
   in a boiling water bath for 15 minutes. (After jars have sealed, remove rings
   to store.)
3. This is great on whole wheat toast, raisin bread (p. 32), cinnamon-raisin bread
   (p. 425), muffins (p. 34-36), shortcake and spice cakes (p. 185-187), and
   pancakes (p. 26-28).

FRUIT DESSERTS

FRESH FRUIT SALAD

Prepare ripe fruit:

oranges, grapefruits, tangerines: peel, break into sections, cut into pieces with a
  sharp, serrated knife

apples: peel if not organic, remove core, cut into pieces

stone fruit (peaches, nectarines, apricots, plums): cut into pieces

bananas: slice

kiwifruit: peel and cut into pieces

pears: cut in quarters lengthwise, remove core, cut into pieces

melon: cut into sections, cut through to rind, remove from rind with knife or spoon

berries: leave small berries whole, slice large strawberries

cherries: halve and pit

pineapple: remove crown, cut in half, cut each half into sections, cut through
  to rind, then remove pieces all at once with knife

*guavas, mangos, papayas, passion fruit, persimmons, pomegranates, and other
  tropical fruits:* great if you can get them

Combine in a bowl. Toss with orange juice to prevent browning.

Fresh Fruit With ...

Use any combination of soy yogurt or soymilk, rice syrup, and/or tahini as a
  dressing for any fruit, combination of a few fruits, or portions of fruit salad.

BAKED APPLES

apples, peeled if not organic
raisins, currants, chopped dates, and/or cranberries
rice syrup or fruit-only jam
cinnamon

1. Preheat oven to 350°.
2. Core apples from the top down, not quite all the way through.
3. Place in baking pan with about ½ inch of water. Put fruit, rice syrup or jam,
   and cinnamon in the centers.
4. Cover (use tin foil if the pan has no lid—you can rinse and reuse it) and bake
   45 minutes, or until soft.

Baked Pears

1. Cut pears lengthwise into halves or quarters and cut out cores—a serrated grapefruit spoon works well for this.
2. Leave plain or sprinkle with any combination of lemon juice, ground ginger, rice syrup, and raisins or currants.
3. Place in pan with ½ inch of water, cover, and bake 30-40 minutes.

STEAMED APPLES AND/OR PEARS

1. Core as many apples (and/or halve and remove core from as many pears) as will fit in a pan. If the fruits are not organic, peel them as well.
2. Place in about ½ inch of boiling water, cover, and steam 10-20 minutes, depending on how soft you want them. Make a lot of these to accompany pancakes (p. 26-28).
3. Save the liquid—it's fresh fruit juice.
4. Mashed steamed apples or pears can double as applesauce or pearsauce, so it's a good idea to make extra. Store in refrigerator or freezer until you need it.

STEAMED APPLES WITH DUMPLINGS

4 cups (about 1 pound) dried apples, or 8 cups sliced, peeled fresh apples
1½ cups whole wheat pastry flour
1½ tsp baking powder
2 tblsp rice syrup
about ⅓ cup plain or vanilla soymilk
cinnamon
raisins, currants, unsweetened carob chips (optional)

1. For dried apples, soak in a wide skillet in 1 quart water for 30 minutes. Bring to a boil, cover, and simmer 30 minutes, or until tender.
2. For fresh apples, place slices in a wide skillet with water to just cover bottom of pan, cover, and cook 6-8 minutes, until beginning to soften.
3. Combine flour and baking powder in a bowl. Add rice syrup and stir in soymilk to make a stiff batter.
4. Drop by tablespoons onto the simmering apple mixture. Sprinkle with cinnamon.
5. Cover tightly and cook on medium-low heat for 20 minutes.
6. Place in bowls while still hot.

If you like, adorn with raisins or currants and/or carob chips, and pour more soymilk over.

APPLESAUCE OR PEARSAUCE OR APPLE-PEARSAUCE

1. Peel and cut up apples and/or pears.
2. Place in a saucepan with just a tiny bit of water.
3. Cover, heat slowly to a boil, reduce heat, and simmer until fruit is so soft it becomes sauce when stirred with a fork.

If you make extra, store in refrigerator or freezer until you need it.

RAW APPLESAUCE

1. Peel and core apples and cut into large chunks.
2. Purée in a blender or food processor.
3. Add lemon, lime or orange juice to help prevent browning, although browning affects neither flavor nor nutrition.

KUZU FRUIT SALAD

1. Stir in 1 tblsp kuzu (p. 20) for each cup of cold fruit juice.
2. Stir constantly as you bring it to a boil.
3. Add small pieces of fruit as it begins to thicken.
4. Pour into dishes and chill, or eat warm.

AGAR (KANTEN) GEL

Agar is a natural plant gelatin derived from sea vegetables, available in bars, strands, flakes and powder.

1. Use 1 tblsp agar flakes or grated kanten bar (or powder—see below) for every 2 cups apple juice or other clear fruit juice. Stir agar flakes into juice in a saucepan. Bring to a boil, then simmer 2-3 minutes, stirring until flakes are dissolved.
2. Pour into one bowl, individual serving bowls, or a lightly oiled mold or one that's been immersed in cold water. Cool to thicken.
3. To unmold, immerse mold to the top in warm water, lightly loosen the edge with a knife, and turn the mold from side to side. Place a serving dish on top and invert.
4. If using agar powder, stir into boiling juice and simmer 10 minutes. Let stand until it gels, then chill.

Fruit Gel

1. Prepare agar gel. Let sit 10 minutes.
2. Then fold in 1 cup berries or chopped fruit, such as peaches, nectarines, apricots, apples, or bananas.
3. Let set in refrigerator about 30 minutes.

Grain Beverage-Apple Gel

2 tblsp dry grain beverage (p. 217)	3 cups sliced peeled apples
3 cups boiling water	½ cup raisins or currants
3 tblsp agar flakes	1 tblsp rice syrup

1. Place grain beverage in a pan and stir in boiling water.
2. Stir in agar flakes. Reduce heat and simmer 10 minutes, stirring occasionally.
3. Add apples, raisins, and rice syrup, and cook 5 more minutes.
4. Pour into a mold or serving dishes and refrigerate until firm, at least 1 hour.

TOFU SHAKE

Purée in a blender or food processor:

1 cup apple juice or any fruit juice
1 banana and/or other fresh fruit
8 oz tofu

SOYMILK SHAKE

Purée in a blender or food processor:

1 cup total fruit juice and plain, vanilla, or carob soymilk, or soy yogurt
1 banana and/or other fresh fruit
carob powder (optional)

FROZEN DESSERTS

FROZEN FRUIT AND SOYMILK DESSERTS

You can easily prepare an infinite variety of delicious and wholly nutritious frozen desserts. The secret of these creamy delights is to simultaneously freeze and beat air into the blended ingredients.

Pour the chilled mixture (see below) into a shallow tray or baking pan, and put it in the freezer. Every 20 minutes, remove the pan from the freezer and stir. Continue until your treat is entirely frozen. If it becomes too hard to scoop, let it soften awhile in the refrigerator.

If you have a freezer canister ice cream maker, such as "Chillfast," it's extremely quick and easy. Leave the inner cylinder in the freezer until your dessert blend is ready. Then, put the ring on the chilled cylinder and place the cylinder in the outer case. Set the blade in place and quickly pour in the blended ingredients. Cover, attach handle, and turn intermittently, and in both directions, for about 10 minutes.

If two people are sharing, you can each take a spoon and eat it right out of the chilled pan or cylinder. That way, it won't melt.

If you do spoon it into serving bowls or over pie slices, crisps, crunches, cobblers, etc., you must serve and eat it without delay! It's worth this small inconvenience to avoid the hundreds of chemical additives used to process commercial ice cream and the high fat and sugar content of both mainstream and so-called natural ice creams.

Sherbet

Use any fruit juice or combination of fruit juices.

Soy Cream and Frozen Soygurt

Place berries, chopped peaches, or any other chopped fruit or combination, in a 1-quart measuring cup. If you like, add a handful of unsweetened carob chips. Pour in fruit juice and vanilla or plain soymilk or soy yogurt in any proportion to make a total of 2½ cups of soy cream/frozen soygurt.

A fresh or frozen banana or half banana, chopped and added to the mix, contributes both flavor and a creamy consistency. (Thaw the frozen banana for a moment before chopping.)

You can also add one or two teaspoons of carob powder.

Melon Ice

Purée in a blender or food processor:

5-6 cups seeded, peeled, and cubed ripe honeydew, cantaloupe, or watermelon
2 tblsp fresh lime juice
1 tsp grated lime peel

Make it creamier by replacing some of the melon with vanilla soymilk.

FROZEN BANANAS

Peel bananas, remove strings, cut in half, and place in the freezer.
    Eat plain for dessert, or thaw a minute and chop for use in soy cream (p. 209).

SNACKS

NIBBLES

BEVERAGES

NIBBLES

BAKED CHICKPEAS

1. Soak dried chickpeas overnight in plenty of water. Drain, rinse, cover with fresh water, and bring to a boil.
2. Simmer, partly covered, until tender, about an hour. Or, cover dried chickpeas with water, bring to a boil, reduce heat, cover, and simmer 3 hours. Or, used canned chickpeas.
3. Drain well, spread on nonstick or lightly oiled baking pan in a single layer, and bake 30-40 minutes at 350° until dry and browned. Shake occasionally while baking to brown evenly.
4. For a more tender, flaky texture, freeze the beans after cooking and bake later.

ROASTED SOYBEANS

3 cups whole dry soybeans, rinsed and soaked 6 hours

1. Drain soybeans well and pat dry.
2. Spread in one layer on large unoiled baking pans or sheets. Place in unheated oven, then roast at 200°-250° for 2-2½ hours, until beans are light brown. Shake pans once every 15 minutes for the first hour, then every 30 minutes. Don't let the beans turn dark brown. While beans are still slightly soft, remove from oven and cool.

BAKED PUMPKIN OR WINTER SQUASH SEEDS

Wash the seeds in a colander to remove strings. Put seeds in a small open pan. Next time you use the oven, bake them until dry and just beginning to brown, about 15 minutes, shaking or stirring occasionally. To conserve energy, wait until you're using the toaster oven or oven for something else. The temperature doesn't matter: hotter will take less time than cooler. Just watch them carefully if they're in a hot oven. We usually dry and bake them in stages, using the residual heat from toaster oven or oven that's just been turned off. Or set the pan on top of your wood stove or other heater.

POPCORN

Use a hot air popper. Re-pop unpopped kernels.

Sprinkle the popped corn with hot sauce in a large bowl and toss with a fork or your hands.

Put it in a large brown bag and take it to the movies.

ROASTED CHESTNUTS

Using a special chestnut knife or any small knife, make crosses on the tops and bottoms of fresh chestnuts.

Place on a dry baking sheet and bake at 300° for about 15 minutes, until soft and easy to peel. Peel as soon as they're cool enough to handle, or peeling becomes more difficult.

Or, place in a steamer and steam over hot water until soft, also about 15 minutes.

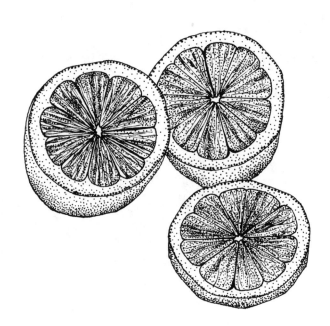

BROILED GRAPEFRUIT

Preheat broiler.

Halve grapefruits, remove seeds, and place cut side up on a pan. If you don't have grapefruit spoons, cut around the sections now with a grapefruit knife or other small knife.

Broil about 5 minutes; watch so they don't get too brown.

Place in small bowls. Spread on rice syrup and/or sprinkle with crystalline vitamin C.

TOFU "CREAM CHEESE"

12 oz tofu, squeezed (p. 7)	garlic, pressed or finely chopped (optional)
2 tblsp lemon juice	1 tsp dried dill weed (optional)
⅛ tsp white pepper	

Purée in a blender. Good on plain or toasted wholegrain bread or bagels, crackers, etc., or as a dip for raw vegetables.

Okara "Feta"

Mash okara (see p. 9) with lemon or lime juice, tamari, tahini, mirin, white and black pepper, curry powder, and dried parsley.

Like tofu "cream cheese," it's good on plain or toasted wholegrain bread or bagels, crackers, etc., and as a dip for raw vegetables. Or use it in place of feta cheese in an early summer spinach salad.

Instant Snacks

- ❀ fresh fruit
- ❀ raw vegetables—plain or dipped in mustard, chutney, soy cream cheese (p. 11), tofu cream cheese (p. 214), or other dip
- ❀ shortening-free hard pretzels dipped in mustard
- ❀ rice cakes with rice syrup and sliced fruit
- ❀ gorp—combine in a bowl: raisins or currants, unsweetened carob chips, and faultless fat- and sugar-free cereal, such as crunchy wheat and barley cereal or Oatios
- ❀ rolled oats with raisins, currants, and/or fresh fruit—dry or with cold water, juice, applesauce (p. 207), soymilk, or soy yogurt (p. 10)

BEVERAGES

Fizzy Water

A seltzer maker (soda siphon), with carbon dioxide cartridges (which are recyclable) will keep you supplied with carbonated water, just like club soda. Put some lemon or lime juice in your glass first. (Squeeze the juice from a whole lemon or lime and store in a small shaker-cap bottle in the refrigerator.) Or try a few drops of pure vanilla (cream soda!) or almond extract or any natural flavoring.

To make a cooling summertime spritzer, mix carbonated water with fruit juice in any ratio.

JUICER JUICES

A masticating juicer extracts more nutrition and flavor than a centrifugal type.

Prepare vegetables and fruits according to the manufacturer's instructions. Favorites are carrot, apple, apple-carrot, and apple-pear.

Make a lot at one time and freeze the extra in 1- or 2-cup reusable plastic containers. Label them.

Don't trash or even compost the pulp! Apple and pear pulp can be used as applesauce or pearsauce. Carrot pulp is an instant substitute in any recipe that calls for grated carrots, such as salads, muffins, and potato kugel. Pulp stores well in the refrigerator and freezes well, too.

Winter Sunshine Drink

The proportions are 1 cup tomato juice, ¼ cup sprouts (p. 11), such as alfalfa, red clover, or lentil, and a dash of lemon juice. Chop sprouts and mix by hand, or use a blender or food processor.

Grain Beverages

Bambu, Cafix, Inka, Pero, Roma are all delicious caffeine-free instant grain beverages made from some combination of barley, rye, chicory, malt, beets, and/or figs.

Place one rounded or heaping teaspoon in a cup or mug, pour boiling water over, and stir. In summer, you can use ice-cold water.

You may prefer it sweetened with rice syrup and/or lightened with plain or vanilla soymilk or soymilk powder.

Hot Carob

Place one rounded or heaping teaspoon of carob powder in a cup or mug, pour boiling water over, and stir. Add some rice syrup and plain or vanilla soymilk or soymilk powder.

Soy Nog

Stir 1 tsp rice syrup and ⅛ tsp nutmeg into each cup of warm or hot plain or vanilla soymilk.

HERB TEAS

We used to scoop our tea herbs from big glass jars at the coop and use a bamboo strainer for a mug or two and a teaball for a teapot. We drank them plain or in combination for their flavor or for relief: peppermint for an upset stomach, chamomile for frayed nerves, slippery elm bark root for a sore throat, rosehips for a cold.

Now most of the big glass jars, except for the ones containing herbs with widely accepted medicinal value, have been replaced with those colorful boxes of tea bags containing single herbs and all kinds of blends: fruity, minty, soothing, spicy. Pour boiling water over the tea bag in a cup or mug and let steep: the longer, the stronger. Or use several teabags and steep in a teapot. For iced tea, boil water, pour over tea, steep, and pour over ice in a cup or mug. (Put a metal spoon in the cup to prevent cracking.)

The decision process is the same—finding a good match between the tea and the time of day, your mood, and the food or dessert the tea will accompany.

You can boost your intake of vitamin C by dissolving a small amount of crystalline C in a fruit-flavored tea every morning at breakfast.

You can make a large amount of tea without boiling any water. Use one tea bag per cup of good tap water, purified water, or bottled water in a pitcher or jar. Cover and place in the sun for a few hours, to make "sun tea," or outside overnight to make "moon tea," or in the refrigerator for at least an hour, to make iced tea. (To make a large amount of instant iced tea, boil the water, steep in a pot, and pour over ice.)

If possible, get unbleached tea bags; bleached ones may contain traces of dioxin.

CAMPING

You can enjoy delicious, healthful , "all-you-can-eat," quick-and-easy food while hiking, bicycling, or canoeing without any overpackaged, undersized, overpriced, prepared "camping foods." All it takes is access to a good natural foods coop or store and some planning.

BREAKFAST MIX

Unless conditions are very cold, backpacking, canoeing, and bicycle-travel breakfast (and dessert) is always the same and always a treat. Before setting out, pour all the standard cold breakfast cereals into a big bowl or bucket and mix them together. The foundation of the breakfast mix is bulk rolled oats. Depending on how long you plan to be out, add several boxes each of generic "crunchy wheat and barley cereal" (much cheaper than the original Grape-Nuts) and crumbled shredded wheat, and smaller quantities of the less-dense puffed grains, cornflakes, Oaties, and other sugar- and honey-free packaged cereals from the coop or natural foods store. You can mix in a good count of raisins or currants now, or keep them with the other dried fruits (see below). Then portion the mix into reused, packable-size double plastic bags and seal them tightly with their zip locks or twisters.

A few handfuls in a Sierra-style camping cup with water (heat the water on a cool morning) is instant breakfast. Seconds and thirds seem to refill the cups spontaneously, so take care that you aren't depleting rations you'll need towards the end of your trip. Count out camping-cupfuls for the number of breakfasts (and desserts) you're relying on the mix to sustain you (two or three cupfuls for breakfast plus one or two for dessert), and add some extra in case the trip is unexpectedly lengthened.

You can also prepare ahead to have fruit and fruit juice with your breakfast every day. Before leaving home, use knife and/or scissors, or food processor, to finely chop a mixture of different kinds of dried fruit. (Put raisins or currants in whole.) Pack them in double small plastic bags, well sealed with zip locks or twisters. As part of your evening routine on the trail, place some of this mix in a small plastic container, pour water over to nearly fill the container, cover tightly, and keep it protected with the rest of your food stores. By morning, you'll have soft, plumped fruit to spoon over your cereal mix and plenty of sweet nectar to pour over it.

Couscous can prevent premature depletion of your breakfast mix supply. Soak some overnight (water:couscous is 3:1) along with the dried fruit or in its own plastic container, and combine it in your cup with the dry mix in the morning.

Carry small containers, such as plastic vitamin bottles, of crystalline vitamin C and spirulina (blue-green algae) powder and sprinkle a spoon-handle-end's worth of each on the first bowl of the day for extra nutrition.

We like this breakfast mix so much, we took no other food except pre-measured bags of it on a six-day "tramp" (Kiwi for hike) on the Abel Tasman Track, South Island, New Zealand, during the southern hemisphere summer.

Hot Breakfasts

Because you're probably eager to pack and get going in the morning, you'll rarely cook breakfast. But it's good to have some hot-breakfast alternatives with you if you decide to stay at the same campsite an extra day or want or need something hot on a chilly day. Carry small amounts of quick-cooking Wheatena or grits (with the instructions cut out or copied); you can also cook for porridge the cornmeal and couscous you're carrying for dinner grains.

Water boils quickly in a teapot for herb tea bags (packed in a small sealed plastic bag) or a grain beverage (packed in a small plastic container). Bambu, Cafix, Inka, Pero, and Roma are delicious caffeine-free instant beverages made from combinations of barley, rye, chicory, malt, beets, and figs. Place one rounded or heaping teaspoon in a cup, pour boiling water over, and stir. You may prefer it sweetened with rice syrup and/or lightened with soymilk powder (also packed in a small plastic container.). Two tablespoons of miso in a cup of boiling water (thin miso first in a small amount of boiling water) and instant miso soup mixes make other warming and nourishing cool-morning starters.

You can carry bagels on the first few days of a trip. These can be split, speared with a fork, and toasted over the camping stove. Then spread with fruit-only jam or rice syrup (packed in camping-food squeeze tubes).

LUNCH

The ideal trail lunch tastes good, is healthful, lightweight, and easy to access in your pack, requires minimum prep and clean-up time, and can be eaten anywhere, even behind or under a makeshift windbreak or raincover. Wholegrain, shortening-free crackers, such as some types of Wasa or RyVita, with tahini and rice syrup and/or fruit-only jam, accompanied by dried fruit, fit all the criteria.

Before leaving on a hiking or canoe trip, make a mix of unsulphured, no-sugar-added dried fruit, such as apples, apricots, banana chips, dates, figs, nectarines, papaya, peaches, pears, pineapple, and/or prunes, and divide it among several double plastic bags. Wrap packages of crackers in double plastic bags to protect against moisture and crushing. Rice cakes are OK: they're light but crumble easily and take up a lot of space; you can tie them to the outside of your pack.

During the morning camp-breaking, put all the "lunch stuff" in one place toward the top of your pack: a bag of dried fruit, a package of crackers, and squeeze tubes of tahini, rice syrup, and fruit-only jam. An opened empty cracker wrapper (carry it out) or an easily-wiped-clean plastic bag or two serve as a placemat, and no utensils are needed. The beverage, appropriately, is purified water from water bottles. Wipe your hands and placemat with a damp rag.

Instant hummus (p. 202) on crackers is another quick trail lunch.

Leftovers from dinner are a rarity on an outdoor trip, but occasionally the eye is actually bigger than the stomach, and you are surprised to discover you can't eat it all. Packed in a plastic container, these are a welcome addition to the standard lunch. Keep forks handy.

On bicycle trips and short hiking and canoe trips, or the first few days of longer ones, you can enjoy the luxury of fresh foods for lunch. Less-fragile fruit, such as apples and oranges, and wholegrain, shortening- and sweetener-free bagels and those small, dense, thinly-sliced loaves that we call "keeper" bread (found in the deli section of some supermarkets, near the pita), take the place of the dried fruit and crackers. Or bake brown rice bread (p. 39) in advance. It's is a very dense and chewy bread, perhaps similar to the waybread Bilbo and the dwarves carried on their ponies into the Misty Mountains.

DINNER

ONE-POT DINNERS

An infinite variety of filling and flavorful backpacking, canoeing, and bicycling dinners can be made by combining quick-cooking grains (to conserve camping-stove fuel) with dried vegetables, legumes, and seasonings. Depending on how much water you use, dinner can be either stew or soup.

The fastest-cooking grains, along with their water: grain ratios and prep methods are:

bulgur wheat (2:1)
Stir boiling water over, cover, let sit about 15 minutes.

couscous (3:1)
Stir boiling water over, cover, let sit about 15 minutes.

quick brown rice
Take the directions with you: different brands have different proportions and cooking times (not more than 10 minutes).

Or, make your own: Roast brown rice as for rice cream cereal (p. 24). At the campsite, place in a pot with twice as much water, cover and bring to a boil. Lower heat, simmer about 15 minutes, then stir, re-cover, and let sit off heat. Pre-soaking will decrease cooking time. Prepared this way, rice will quadruple in volume.

rolled rye, wheat, and soy flakes (2:1)
Stir into boiling water, simmer and stir 5-10 minutes.

buckwheat groats (kasha) (2:1)

Stir into boiling water, cover and simmer on lowest heat 10-15 minutes.

angel hair and ramen noodles

These cook in boiling water in five minutes or less. Rice vermicelli doesn't even need to be cooked; just soak in hot water and drain.

If you don't have the ratios and prep methods memorized, record them in your journal or keep them on slips of paper between the double bags that hold each grain.

Another one-pot dinner must-have is dried vegetable mix, such as Frontier Hearty Vegetable Stew Blend. You can also bring separate dried vegetables; maybe your favorites are available in bulk. Dried onions are basic to many entrées on the trail, just as fresh ones are at home. Sea vegetables add a distinctive flavor. They can be snipped or crumbled at home. Pack dried vegetables in small plastic bags and keep them together with other small bags of dinner ingredients in a larger, heavier plastic bag. If the bags aren't transparent, or the contents may not be readily identifiable, be sure to label them.

High-protein dry soy foods add more heartiness and nutrition. Freeze-dried tofu, texturized vegetable protein (TVP), made from defatted soy flakes, and soy grits or granules, made from toasted coarsely ground soybeans, can all be soaked in advance or reconstituted in the pot for at least 10 minutes as the water boils.

You can buy freeze-dried tofu at a coop or natural foods store, or you can make it (below). Since the tofu is broken into pieces and crumbled anyway for use in camping dinners, TVP and/or soy grits or granules may be a less expensive and more convenient choice. The trade-off is that TVP and grits/granules lack the chewy, satisfying "mouth-feel" of reconstituted freeze-dried tofu.

Seasonings are the finishing touch. Reused small prescription containers are good for packing herbs, spices, and blends (film canisters may transfer toxins); squeeze tubes for miso and tahini. You can probably accumulate a few tiny plastic containers to reuse for hot sauce and tamari.

There's no one correct way to prepare a one-pot dinner. Use your judgement in adapting the cooking requirements of the different components. Add the grain first or after the water boils, depending on its requirements. (For use in soup, the couscous and bulgur don't have to soak in boiled water; to keep to one pot, just stir them in as the water boils.) In general, put dried vegetables and soy foods into the water right away to give them time to reconstitute. Bring to a boil, simmer, and stir. Keep covered between stirrings. Add more water if needed. Add herbs to the pot and other seasonings right to your bowl.

Freeze-dried Tofu

Prepare, freeze, and reconstitute a pound block of tofu according to the instructions on p. 14.

Preheat oven to 170°.

Arrange the reconstituted tofu on a baking sheet, leaving space around each piece. Bake about 2 hours, until slices are crisp and dry. Remove and cool. The tofu should be dry, crisp, firm, and light beige. Store in sealed plastic bags in a cool dry place and use within 3 months.

The traditional method for making freeze-dried tofu is to freeze tofu slices by setting them on a board on the snow overnight in winter. They are brought inside to dry for a week, then returned outside to freeze each night and thaw each day for 2-4 weeks.

Enhanced Ramen

Ramen—packaged quick-cooking noodles with broth mix—can be augmented with your one-pot dinner ingredients to make a much heartier and more filling soup, and more of it! Get coop or natural foods store ramen, such as Westbrae, with wholegrain noodles that were steamed, not fried.

Use a quart or more of water, instead of the 2-3 cups suggested on the package. Put dried vegetables and soy foods (p. 223-224) into the water as soon as possible after you begin dinner prep. Coarsely broken fu (sheets of dried wheat gluten) or a small amount of a quick-cooking grain are other good enhancers. Cover the pot and bring to a boil, stirring occasionally. Add more water if needed. When the water boils, simmer until everything is rehydrated. Break up the ramen noodles as you stir them in, and cook another 2-3 minutes. Meanwhile, thin miso in some of the hot broth. When the noodles are ready, add the miso to the soup along with the contents of the broth packet.

Other Soup-Based Dinners

Dehydrated vegetable powders, which are available in bulk, and instant soup mixes can be foundations for soup-and-cracker dinners. Vegetable powders call for about one tablespoon per cup of water. Pea powder needs about 5 minutes simmering time; basic vegetable broth powder needs 1-2 minutes, and tomato powder needs none. The directions that come with soup mixes are either to just place in a cup or bowl, add boiling water, and stir, or to cook for several minutes or longer.

But to satisfy your appetite after a day of hiking, canoeing, or cycling, use more water than the powder or mix directions call for, and as you bring the water to a boil, add other one-pot dinner ingredients: a small amount of a quick-cooking grain, dried land and sea vegetables and soy foods, herbs, and miso. Make sure the dried foods are fully rehydrated before you declare the soup done. Stir in the soup mix according to the timing in the directions; if it's the mix-in-a-cup type, add it to the pot anyway. Some examples:

pea soup
  Soak dried onions and potatoes in the water as you bring it to a boil before adding the pea powder.

creamy tomato-rice soup
  Use quick brown rice, soy powder, and tomato powder.

miso soup
  Soak dried vegetables, tofu, etc. in the water as you bring it to a boil. Thin miso in some of the hot broth, then stir in.

tomato-vegetable soup
  Use a combination of tomato powder, vegetable broth powder, dried vegetables, and any other additions you're inspired to include.

CORNMEAL, BEANS, AND SALSA

This is a three-potter, but quick and easy.

Pre-cooked bean flakes—black beans and refried pinto beans—are available in bulk at natural foods coops and stores. First, boil water for the beans in a covered pot or teapot: 2 cups of water for every 1½ cups of beans. Measure the beans into another pot, and when the water boils, pour it over the beans, stir well, cover, and let sit 5 minutes.

Now boil water for the cornmeal in a larger pot. The ratio is 3 cups water for every cup of cornmeal. Lumping is not a problem if you dissolve the cornmeal first in an equal amount of cold water, then stir into the boiling water. For example, boil two cups of water and stir one cup of dry cornmeal into one cup of cold water until the mixture is smooth. Add the cornmeal to the boiling water, return to a boil, and cook briefly, stirring. Cover to keep it warm.

In the third pot or container, make the sauce. Combine tomato powder and water to desired consistency, about ¼ cup powder with each cup of water. Add hot sauce or chili powder for trailside salsa.

You're ready to eat! Put cornmeal in bowls, top with beans, and pour sauce over all. Don't forget to put some Beano drops on your first bite.

INSTANT TABOULI

This is ideal for an evening when you've been delayed by conversation or a jump in the brook, or misjudged distance or conditions and arrive at your camp spot later than you'd hoped. Like its fresh counterpart, instant tabouli (available in bulk at natural foods coops and stores) contains parsley, onions, garlic, lemon, herbs, and spices, all in dried form, along with bulgur wheat.

The only missing ingredient is tomatoes, which you can supply. At home, snip dried tomatoes or chop them in a food processor, and carry in a small bag along with the tabouli mix.

Place equal parts of tabouli mix and water in one of your camping pots. Stir in a handful of chopped dried tomatoes. Cover and let sit 30 minutes or longer, while you organize your campsite and savor your surroundings. Use crackers as scoops.

INSTANT HUMMUS

This saves the day on those rare occasions when things have gone so wrong and you are so late and tired, and possibly wet, arriving at your camp spot that you don't even feel like bothering with dinner. Like its fresh counterpart, instant hummus (available in bulk at natural foods coops and stores) contains chickpeas, tahini, garlic, spices, and lemon, all in dried form.

Place hummus mix in a bowl, container, or small pot. Add water and stir. The longer it sits, the thicker it gets, so you may need to add more water. Spread on crackers, perhaps garnished with dried onions.

Rojo's Best Burgers and Buns

8 burgers

1 heaping cup cooked (or soaked) couscous (p. 222)
for car camping:
2 cups steamed vegetables, such as finely chopped garlic; chopped onion,
   carrots, summer squash, and celery; and corn
for backpack, bicycle, and canoe camping:
1 cup mixed dried vegetables
½ cup rolled oats: soft, baby, or quick are best.
4 ounces tofu (from aseptic package)
dried parsley, basil, and celery seeds

Mix and mash everything together, form into burgers, and fry over a campfire on a sesame-oiled grill. Carry oil in a tiny well-sealed unbreakable container. (Sesame is the least perishable cooking oil.) The grill can be improvised from a 14- by 24-inch sheet of standard aluminum flashing, folded in half to carry in your pack and unfolded when you need it. Wait for a low-flame, hot-coals fire. Check frequently with a fork or flipper, turn when brown, and continue cooking on the other side.

8 buns

Combine 2 cups whole wheat bread flour and 2 teaspoons baking powder. Stir in just enough water to make a stiff dough. Form into buns and bake over a campfire, flipping when bottom is browned. For an oven effect, bake on half the flashing and fold the other half over. (If you want to make them at home, place them on a baking sheet and bake in a 350° oven until nicely browned, about 15 minutes on each side.)

Split open buns. Spread with miso and tahini or mustard, or use tomato sauce— perhaps blended with chili powder or hot sauce, ketchup-like sauce (p. 134), or salsa. Depending on where you are and what you have, enjoy as is or top burgers with fluffy sprouts and lettuce, and sliced onions, tomatoes, and mushrooms. Or put the burgers on wholegrain bread or in whole wheat pita.

BEVERAGES

Unfortunately, the reality is that we have to assume all groundwater to be contaminated. It's essential to carry and use a small-pored water filter. For breakfast-cereal water and thirst-quenching through the day, use filtered water stored in polycarbonate water bottles, which don't impart a plastic taste to the water.

For cold mornings and evening dessert, carry herb tea bags, well-secured in labeled plastic bags, and a grain beverage (p. 217) in a small reused container. You can use carob powder and soy powder (1 heaping teaspoon of each per cup) and rice syrup to make hot "chocolate."

FREEZE-DRIED WATER

Open the package and empty into water bottle or other container. Add water to fill.

DESSERT

Ever-versatile rolled oats, or your oat-based dry breakfast mix, sprinkled with raisins or currants and eaten dry or with water, cold or hot, depending on season and location, nicely rounds off y our evening meal. Or, soak some couscous and chopped dried fruit when you arrive and have it in place of all or some of the oats or mix.

Edible wild berries picked along the trail and stored in a plastic container provide an unexpected dessert treat. Mix them with your oats and couscous, squish them on crackers for instant jam (make wild cranberry jam by cooking cranberries briefly with a bit of water and rice syrup), or invent your own spontaneous creation with whatever's in your packs. Try to save some berries for breakfast.

If you want to get more involved, you can make instant tapioca pudding. Prepare it before dinner, so it has a chance to thicken a bit more before you eat it. If you take the time to make the dry pudding mix at home, you'll be very pleased with yourself when the time comes to cook it. The proportions are 1 part carob powder with 2 parts granulated tapioca and 4 parts soy powder; for example, ¼ cup carob powder, ½ cup tapioca, and 1 cup soy powder.

In a pot, stir a heaping ½ cup of pudding mix into 2 cups of water. Let soak 5 minutes. Bring to a boil, stirring. Reduce heat to medium, and cook and stir about a minute. Let sit until thick. Then add 2 or more tablespoons of rice syrup.

It's also pleasant to munch on dried fruit or unsweetened carob chips as you relax in your sleeping bag.

INDEX